DESTRUCTION OF INNOCENCE

Shane Roberta Farmer

**Grosvenor House
Publishing Limited**

This book is published by
Grosvenor House Publishing Ltd
Link House
140 The Broadway, Tolworth, Surrey, KT6 7HT.
www.grosvenorhousepublishing.co.uk

A CIP record for this book
is available from the British Library

ISBN 978-1-83615-266-8

FOREWORD

Shane died unexpectedly on 6 November 2021. She had told us she was writing a book, which she said was a memoir, and we would probably be surprised by some of the revelations in it. She hoped one day it would be published, and that any proceeds should go to a Dog Charity, so when we found her manuscript, we set about transcribing it as accurately as we could.

PART ONE – DESTRUCTION OF INNOCENCE

Shane tells about her life as a child and her young adulthood; As an only child she spent a great deal of time on her own, with only her thoughts for company. Her Mum had to move around the country to find work, so Shane found it difficult to make friends as she was never at one school long enough to form lasting friendships. For many years her father was poorly, which added to the stress and the need for Shane's mother to provide for the family.

Even as a child, she understood her Mum had to work, which at times meant moving, but Shane found it difficult to understand why her Mum never explained what was happening. And so, her problem with trust started at a very early age, as she was never sure where or when they would be moving or for how long. There was often no time to say goodbye to friends, and so it was easier not to form close bonds with any of her school mates so the wrench of leaving them behind was not too hard to bear. Her Dad was the only person she ever truly trusted, and she found leaving him behind when she had to move with her Mum difficult to cope with. She never doubted that her Dad loved her, even though he couldn't travel with them, she knew he missed her just as much as she missed him. Because she felt her Mum was not always truthful about the situation regarding both the need to move to find work and her father's illness, over the years she lost trust in her Mum.

This lack of trust would stay with Shane throughout her life.

The second part of the book RUNNING SCARED is Shane's attempt to address her trust issues, talking about relationships and how they affect her personally. But this is Shane's story and it is her perspective that she writes about, so some of what she details may not be factually accurate, rather how she saw them from a trust perspective.

Shane met Grace in 1994 after her relationship with Kelly ended. With her trust in people having been further damaged by Kelly's affair with one of their close friends, Grace seemed like a guardian angel, willing to listen to Shane and to try to help process her problems over her lack of trust. Maybe Shane became obsessed with analysing her feelings, trying to make sense of past events, and perhaps with the right support she may have found an understanding, but as so often happens, life got in the way leaving her confused and bitter with the very person who had tried to help her. Ultimately, Shane and Grace would renew their friendship after their relationship ended, although Shane never resolved her lack of trust in people.

INTRODUCTION

We have all read books, even if it's only been a passage or two, where the author's talent manages to bring to life things that many of us rarely think of, or only ever dream about.

I am not an author and within the realms of possibility I'm never likely to become one, and although I haven't the naturel gift to write, I have still spent the previous five years preparing this book.

It was never a book intended for publication, although if that were to happen someday, I'd be more than honoured, surprised and greatly overwhelmed. In fact, the book fundamentally had a genuine reason for being written and was treated as part of an emotional therapy treatment for myself. My intentions were to use it as a self-help diary in a way to find out and understand how my current mental state had been affected by past events, and to see if I could find the person within me who was not afflicted by mistrust and doubt.

This however wasn't without a major problem. In the first six months of its creation the thought that I could complete my own exorcism through pen and paper brought on a behaviour that I can only describe as being obsessional. The thought of the freedom that it could eventually bring, ruled my waking hours and even my dreams, so much so that as a result it nearly cost me my valued relationship. From that harsh realisation, the book had a time and a place, hence the five years.

The subjects that I have endeavoured to discuss and passionately describe, have come from the heart and not imagination. It has not been an easy journey and at times has been extremely painful but with friends that have supported me, and I thank you all, anything is possible.

The friend that I would like to thank the most, although sadly is no longer with us, is my Dad. Physically he doesn't exist but spiritually he stood by me, cradled me and gave me comfort. At a quiet moment of the day, I truly thank him, I just wish at times he could hear me as a mortal again and not a spirit. God bless you Dad, I love you. xxx

Shane R Farmer

PART ONE

DESTRUCTION OF INNOCENCE

CHAPTER ONE

I brought the car to an abrupt halt, engaged the handbrake, turned off the engine and stared. I sat there for what seemed an eternity, contemplating whether to drive away or stay. After some time looking at the gate, that still hung on a solitary hinge from all those years ago, I found myself being drawn towards it like metal to a magnet.

By now I was all too well aware of the emotions of excitement and fear conflicting with each other. To be honest I feared the consequences of the actions I was about to take, but there was just a little bit of excitement which drove me forward. I was now a woman, forty and in my prime, I had ideas, hopes and dreams but this place in front of me, yet again, was trying to control me, or at least something was. I wanted to turn on my heels and run, but found I couldn't, it was all too late, I was here now. I felt I had once more become a pawn in a sadistic game of chess, it was now a case of survival; I had to find the strength to rid myself of the painful labyrinth of memories and face reality so I could move on with my life. I knew from that moment what had to be done. Firstly, I had to confront myself and then the power that came from beyond the gate.

I knew in my heart it was now or never. As I walked towards the house for the first time in years, my mind and body started to work as they should. I realised the strength I had always had, always wanted but lacked for so long was suddenly deep within me, the time had come. The battle of two forces was about to commence. Win or lose, it didn't matter and more to the point, the end was now clearly visible, my demons would either be put to rest or would haunt me for the rest of my life.

I tried to close the gate behind me but the many changing seasons that it had endured had finally taken its toll. The rotting wood and thickly coated rust on the solitary hinges couldn't withstand another external blow. It fell to the ground with a hollow thud and immediately broke into a pile of splinters and dust. It had served a useful purpose in its youth but now it had decayed through age and lack of care.

The old, cobbled path had changed considerably with time. Nature had taken control as it always does. Instead of being new as I remembered, it had become mature, the rough uniformed edges of the stones were worn smooth and bevelled. An invasion of moss carpeted small areas, with little wild pansies and tufts of couch grass nestling in the small cracks and dips. At the same time, the sun had peeped through the canopy of trees where the leaves had not quite opened enough to prevent its penetration, thus permitting a rainbow of shadows, causing some cobbles to appear matt black and mysterious and others soft shiny amber like watery silk.

I knew my mental and physical awareness of the surroundings had intensified but I didn't quite expect the reaction I was getting. My hands that had been dry earlier had become extremely cold and clammy. My heart was pounding in my chest like a pneumatic drill, it had an undeniable irregular tremor. I didn't want to be here, but I knew I had to be. I felt that someone or something was watching me, but no idea where from. I thought it may be from behind, so I quickly turned, but nothing was there, or at least nothing was visible. I looked to the right, then to the left, back to the front again. By now beads of perspiration were running the very length of my spine and panic was engulfing my whole body. My instinct was to run. I knew if I could get back in the car, I'd be alright. All I had to do was unlock the driver's door, it was simple, but did I really want to run? I'd run away more than twenty years ago; my demons had followed me then and I'd lived a nightmare ever since. Was I really prepared to deny myself the chance of freedom?

I continued walking while trying to retrieve the car keys from my pocket, but it seemed strange. As I walked back towards the car, the path appeared to be narrower with the trees becoming denser. I looked around, in an attempt to gather my bearings. It became obvious I wasn't sure which way to go, so decided to follow the direction I was facing.

The uneasy feeling became stronger so I quickened my pace, but it didn't make much difference. As the sense of urgency increased, I broke into a run. But the faster I ran, the more the intermittent sunrays through the branches blinded me. It penetrated my eyes with such force and velocity it burned. I tried desperately to keep my eyes open but could only manage a squint, even this in the end became unbearable. I stumbled, fell to ground on all fours, got up and I kept running like a frenzied dog hoping my sight and balance would return.

Eventually, I regained my senses and began to calm down. Thank God I was in control once more. Or was I? Of course, I wasn't, I was stupid to think otherwise; my mental clarity, awareness and ability to be rational had been muddled for years and I had lost all pride in my physical appearance. I was middle aged and what had I to show for it. Bigger clothes, a smoker's cough, and each morning a hangover. No, I wasn't in control of my life, I was heading towards self-destruction.

Although I had been blinded by the strong rays of sunlight, as the clouds covered the sun, everything around me instead of being light, had become a misty twilight grey. I wasn't sure where I was "running" to but kept going in the knowledge that I needed to get somewhere. The exertion was making my chest feel tight and painful, with every breath hurting my throat and burning my lungs.

My body felt heavy from the effort of running, every muscle had an intense burning sensation, feeling ready to snap like an overwound spring. The mental and physical punishment was once again the name of the game. I wasn't sure how long it was going to take, or whether I could carry on but knew somehow, I had to.

Through the fear and panic, a burst of adrenaline kicked in, renewing my strength and stamina, and I was able to begin running again. I wanted to look behind me to see what was there, but I dare not stop. I figured to look behind when still running wasn't that difficult when I was younger, why should it be impossible now, but as I began to turn my head towards my right shoulder, I instantly realised this would start an attack of vertigo. I hadn't suffered an attack in quite a few months, why did I have to have one now. Before I had chance to reposition my head, I became completely disorientated. An infusion of shapes without outlines began to spin around, coming closer and closer. I felt sick and wanted to stop running, but suddenly my legs began to buckle and something tall and black loomed directly in front of me.

Suddenly my path was obstructed as I felt a crack and then pain to my head. I slumped to the ground, my vision becoming darker and darker until nothing.

I opened my eyes, slowly at first as I realised it was extremely difficult to focus. I blinked several times to clear the haze that covered my eyes like thick fog. I lay there continually rubbing them, one at a time and then from desperation both together. This finally did the trick and within a few minutes my sight had returned to normal.

Although my sight had recovered, I continued to lie there to gather the remainder of my senses. Looking across to the right, I noticed fresh blades of grass. They stood erect, shiny, unblemished, and virginal. They had been given life just a few days ago, and were now standing there with so much dignity and honour, perfect pure and untouched. They had become a new life. No matter how insignificant to us it may seem, to take life for granted is arrogant as I realised their basic needs were identical to mine. God, the ruler of all nature, created its very existence and yet by its very birth it enters an unequal struggle for survival against its own maker.

I decided to sit up slowly, but instantly had a headache. I brought my knees up to my chest like a child in pain, doing so, I cupped my hands around my head and then lent forward into them. This was my vain attempt to try and cradle my fragile throbbing head from becoming worse and hoping it would make it better. Just as I was about to move my hand, I felt something wet and warm flowing between my thumb and forefinger, shocked at the realisation that in fact it was blood, I investigated further. I didn't need a mirror to confirm my injury, my fingers gave me all the information I required. I felt a large raised area on the right-hand side of my forehead. It followed the line of my recently plucked eyebrows but stopped just before it reached the concave angle of my temple bone. The bulbous hard, painful swelling had a deep wound, from which blood oozed and I could feel gravel and dirt that had stuck to it. I attempted to stop the bleeding and clean it up with a tissue, but it wasn't working. The tissue was sodden with blood and I realised how futile my attempt was. I was already angry, with the world and with myself, I didn't need something like this to happen, there was far too much going on. I threw the tissue to one side and sat and watched the blood drip intermittently onto my T-shirt.

I must have stayed in this position for a considerable time, but I hadn't noticed that the bleeding had stopped until I realised how cold I felt. I suppose I was suffering from shock because my surroundings portrayed a warm summer's day.

Was this a game or reality? Whatever this was, I was confused. I questioned what had happened, where was I in relation to the car, how long had I been there, and most importantly was it all over? Had I done what I set out to do? Was this the end? Had I finally been given my freedom to live at last? I couldn't remember how I had felt when I arrived at the house, all I recalled prior to walking through the gate was a feeling of sheer panic and now, well now quite the opposite. Tranquillity overcomes me, the leaves outstretched from the trees ride on the gentle wind above. With erotic aroma filling the air from the conifer trees and decaying fallen pine needles, to the hurried chit chat of the birds flying overhead. The fledglings of the Great, Blue and Long Tailed tits diving from branch to branch in a playful game of superiority. Was this wonder really playing out in front of me? I pinched myself to see if I was still alive. Yes, I was, thank God.

Still trying to come to terms with this wonderful sight, I leant forward to touch a piece of Ivy and noticed the many shades of green. It grew in abundance at the base of every tree and in its splendour, it crept in all directions taking a foothold at intervals to give stability for its onward growth. Some branches couldn't anchor themselves to the tree, twisting and turning they fell back cascading like a waterfall down to the ground covering the earth, stones, grass and moss as they continued on their way. Hardened to the winter, the ivy provides a place of protection to the many insects and birds who live within its Kingdom, and in the summer the new growth offers safe spaces for nests.

I found myself standing there transfixed, just watching and listening to the sights and sounds that engulfed me. I was in the middle of nature, something so wonderful it was such a shame it had eluded me until now. The thing was, from as far back as I can remember

I had lived only with anger, hatred, disbelief and pain. I spent a lifetime building a brick wall around myself, protecting me and my emotions from any situation. Over the years I've added brick after brick, blocking any gaps in the wall which left me exposed. I allowed myself to become an extremely bitter, uncaring, lonely and volatile woman. Of course, I have loved, but never understood why I couldn't give totally to the person I was with. I always felt when I craved affection, I never received it, but perhaps I did not realise or acknowledge, that had I looked I would have seen the affection there.

I have wanted for so long to be happy, just to love and be loved, to give and receive the support and strength of a partners embrace, to experience the tenderness of a true friend. In my attempt to find happiness, I have managed to isolate myself making it almost impossible for anyone to break through my protective barrier and find the real Shane.

For years I have harboured pain and anger towards several people due to certain circumstances. I believe this has made me a victim not only of my own inadequacies but also because of theirs. But now I wonder if they really were to blame or whether I had allowed it to happen. Was I then and am I still making myself a victim of my own weakness and self-recrimination?

The delightful, peaceful surroundings I found myself in, I knew would not last forever. All the things I have ever loved or given me pleasure, have always been taken away. I have always allowed myself to be drawn in, taken up by the moment not seeing the truth that lies beyond it and ending up being tormented by manipulative behaviour of people. And maybe it is not all their fault, but it leaves me tormented and feeling plagued and abused by the very people I should be able to trust. Sometimes I feel I don't want to live with the loneliness, betrayal and guilt.

In truth, I needed help years ago and the thought that twenty years on I still need help is frightening. Several months earlier, in fact twelve months ago, I'd tried to commit suicide and failed. I knew I wasn't mad, just a very mixed up hurt and scared individual. I suppose I had reached a crossroads in my life and as far as I could see, there were three possible avenues to take. For a long time I studied each route carefully but the direction of each one had the same ending. I had become weak, tired, frustrated and extremely lonely, all I wanted was happiness for once in my life, but it never came. The three avenues had left me with little choice, a small part of me didn't want to die, but the more I thought about an invitation to total peace through death, the more it seemed an option I didn't want to miss.

After failing miserably to take my own life and not receiving any form of counselling from health visitors or suchlike, I found myself sitting outside the church where my father, as a young boy, was in the choir. Day after day I would return, asking God for his protection help and support. I asked him for a sign of hope, it didn't matter how small, just a sign. Through the tears of desperation, I begged for forgiveness for my own sins. I was sorry for the many times of selfish lack of loyalty towards him; I never meant to turn my back on him. Yes, I needed his help now, but I couldn't promise that I could forgive all those that had sinned against me, but I promised I would try.

CHAPTER TWO

I continued to walk along the cobbled path, hoping that eventually I would return to the car. Still confused about what had happened, I realised that my fear had now gone. I felt hypnotised by my surroundings and in a sense, that gave me a feeling of warmth and peace. Ahead, I could see the path leading around to the left and suspected that the gate and car would then be in view from the corner. Saddened having to leave something so wonderful, yet relieved at the same time, I walked on. As I approached and turned the corner, it became all too obvious I wasn't returning to the gate, but in fact, I was looking at the house.

Instantly, reality hit me. Once more, fear and panic surged through every ounce of my body as I stood there, not with a smile on my face, but with tears running and dropping from my cheeks. The pleasure I felt had been taken away from me once again. I looked around to see if I could get back to the feeling of tranquilly, but I knew it had gone. All the lovely flowers, the sweet aroma, it had all disappeared without a trace.

I really didn't want to go forward, although that's why I was here, but where I had just walked from was suddenly lifeless, dark and eerie. I couldn't explain the disappearance and questioned whether I had encountered it at all. As far as I could see, I had one choice that was to carry on. I really didn't like this and began to accept that I had no control in the matter. I was being pushed forward, by what I didn't know, but there was no going back, that was obvious.

I took a deep breath, dried my eyes and started to walk towards the house. It was situated about two hundred yards directly in front of me and twenty years ago when I left, it was up for sale and to this day it still is. The path led right up to the front door and then veered off to the right where it disappeared around the side of the property. A little brick wall edged the path and two gardens, directly in front of each downstairs window. I was pleasantly surprised that the wall remained intact. I must have been thirteen years old when I persuaded Mum to let me build it. Considering I hadn't any experience and hadn't a clue what a spirit level was, I figured I'd done a pretty good job.

The numerous rosebushes which once filled the two gardens were still there but now they had become wild, woody and intermingled with weeds and brambles. The house looked weathered as you would expect. The front door, the old latch type, had taken a battering from the northern winter winds and extreme hot temperatures during the summers.

The windows were dark, empty and had no sign of the draped curtains anywhere. I stood for a while just looking and remembering, I swallowed hard and wished I hadn't come. I wondered what the hell I was doing here and was it all worth it or should I have left it alone. I explored the remaining gardens but eventually came back to the house. The roof which was thatched was covered in moss and in places it had been destroyed altogether.

A momentary glance at the right bedroom window compelled me to look again, I wasn't sure but thought, through the darkness I saw movement, a shadow crossing the window which looked like a person. I focused harder, but I saw nothing this time. I proceeded to the door, telling myself it was just my imagination. I knocked and waited a few minutes but there was no response, of course, there wasn't likely to be, it was empty and had been for years. I placed my hand around the handle with my thumb resting on the latch, and before I had time to think the door swung open. I called out and stupidly expected there to be an answer, in my mind I could still see movement in the bedroom window, if someone was in the house, surely they must have heard.

The door had opened to its full extent and the smell of freshly baked cakes filled my nostrils. I was unsure but walked into the lobby, my shoes making a noise on the quarry tiles. I called out again and instantly walked into a cobweb, I tried quickly to brush it from my face and at the same time tried to understand why I could smell cakes, the odd thing was, it smelt like my mother's baking. This was stupid, it was obvious no one could live here because of its condition and as for my Mum, she had died twenty-one years ago. Standing there for a few minutes trying desperately to come up with a logical explanation, I realised it was in my imagination and told myself to get a grip, pull myself together, if I became weak my resolve would be lost forever.

I thought of Grace; she was the only thing that had kept me going. I loved her and knew she loved me too. She is five foot nothing and no more than a bantamweight, but she had so much strength and determination. For months she has supported me and given me a reason to want to live. At last, I could acknowledge I was gay and for the first time in my life I wasn't ashamed to admit it. I was proud of who I was and of Grace for helping me to accept me. We had a life together, I hoped for a long time to come, if only this nightmare would end. This house held such power over me which I recognised better than Grace did, and although she tried to understand she could never comprehend the effect it had on me. However Grace's love had eased the pain, but I was saddened that she had started to become affected by all of this, and knew she didn't deserve it.

My strength renewed; I closed the door behind me.

The lobby was as I remembered, long, dark and narrow. Halfway down there were two doors directly opposite each other, one giving entrance to the lounge on the left and the other the dining room on the right. At the very end, beyond the half open door, was the kitchen. I was grateful this door was ajar because it enabled me to see a little easier as it let some light into the hall. I could still smell cakes baking and for an instant, I wanted to run into the kitchen and eat one while it was still warm, like I did as a child. I called out but no answer, I slowly walked across towards the door, half expecting it to suddenly open and to hear a voice asking, "can I help you". I pushed the door wide open and as I entered the smell of baking disappeared, replaced by a damp musty aroma.

The room was empty, except for the sink, kitchen units and an old broken bowl on the floor. A thick coating of dust covered the work surfaces and prints showed evidence of where mice had scurried across it. The floor which was not covered but retained the original flag stones, which were wet and dirty. On the drainer were fragments of glass which had come from the broken windowpanes. Because of this, leaves had blown through and started to decay in each corner of the room where they had come to rest. Behind me, the old fridge had bubbles of rust around the door and handle. It was years old, and I remembered once trying to convince Mum to buy a new one but all she would say was, it works and that's all that matters.

So many years had elapsed and to be honest it felt strange, almost as if I were a stranger but one who knew so much about the house and its occupants. I felt consumed by fear, anger and hatred, but also a sense of loyalty to those who used to be here and could no longer answer for their actions.

The kitchen didn't hold many memories, except baking and that's probably why I thought I could smell freshly baked cakes when I entered the house. It wasn't the warm farmhouse type kitchen you think of as being the heart of the home, but utilitarian where food was prepared, washing done and muddy boots left to dry.

I left the door open and returned to the lobby, but now it was showing a sense of powerfulness and familiar possessiveness. I walked some way down the hall when suddenly I was gripped by shock as a portrait of my mother grabbed my attention and inexplicably fell to the ground. The glass shattered and the frame broke in half; I bent down to retrieve it from the floor. Noticing it was face down, I didn't really want to turn it over but I did. My body shook as I looked eye to eye with my mother whom I once loved and respected, but now hated with a passion to the extent I wanted revenge, it didn't matter that she was dead, I wanted her to suffer like I had and still was. I thought of the hours, months and years of anguish I'd spent through her selfish denial of the truth. They say blood is thicker than water but this woman, my mother, had destroyed any thought of what I understood love to be. To be part of her, my mother's daughter, sickened and repulsed me.

I threw the photograph down; mad at myself for picking it up in the first place, I made my way towards the dining room. I stood there frightened to enter. I hadn't always had a dread of this room; it had started to manifest itself in the last twelve months I had lived here. I couldn't believe I still had this problem and decided I would make my way to the stairs instead.

The entrance to the staircase was by means of an archway directly in front of you as you came in through the front door. Still shaken from the experience and angry about the photograph, I climb the stairs and walked into the back bedroom. For years, this had been my room and I had always felt really safe in here. Somehow the room knew everything about me, down to what I thought and what I felt. It was my bolt hole, but more importantly it was my friend. As I stood there, I questioned whether a room could be considered to be your friend, but I realised all those years ago a friend to me wasn't someone I knew, but a place I felt safe in, somewhere I could retreat to and know that no harm could come to me.

I closed the door behind me and walked over to the window and stood there for a while trying to visualise how the garden used to look, but it was overgrown with years of neglect, so it was virtually impossible.

The bedroom although damp and dirty was much how I'd left it. The chair that I'd sat on for so many hours contemplating various things, still occupied the far corner of the room. The more I looked at it, the more I felt compelled to sit on it again but first I had to remove the cobwebs and dust that had settled on it. As I sat down, I realised I'd forgotten just how comfortable the chair really was and before long I started to relax and experience the feeling of being safe and protected, I had always felt in this room. It was the only room in the entire house that held any form of warmth and love. The other rooms were always cold, and even though there may have been a fire burning in the grate, I still felt a chill in the room which I couldn't explain.

Now for the first time in years since leaving this house and in the safety of my room, I can begin to tell you a story about a happy little girl that once had so much love, and all she wanted was to share it with family and friends. This little girl asked for nothing except for love. This is a story of my life until this present day, and how I fought through different situations to seek the love that kept eluding me.

It all began when I was about five and half years old. I had been at my first school for approximately six months, in which time I'd made two friends and settled in quite well. I remembered it was a Tuesday because the following day I'd been invited to my friend's party, but out of the blue, the teacher called me from class to say my mother was waiting to speak to me. I felt so disappointed when she told me we were going away for a while, and I'd miss the party the next day. This was bad enough, but she never gave me chance to say goodbye to my friends. After leaving school we arrived home to find our bags already packed, we were leaving within the hour. There was never any explanation for leaving but I was told Dad was staying to look after the house and shop.

The shop in fact was the dining room which had been converted a few years earlier. Mum told me Dad was staying behind to help him and give him encouragement back onto his feet and eventually back to work. I was far too young to understand the reason why, but he had suffered an illness called T.B. Meningitis, which at the time had a five percent survival rate but bless him he had pulled through and was working towards recovery.

The rest of Tuesday was spent travelling, and Wednesday was the first day of a new chapter in my life and I hated it. I'd woken up in a cold unfamiliar place miles from home, and I didn't know where my mom was. I still wanted to go to my friend's party and wanted my Dad. Within twenty-four hours my life had been ripped apart and I didn't know why.

We had moved to a place called Punnett's town. It was a sleepy little village in West Sussex, with a population of around five hundred. Ten miles further on was Hastings and Eastbourne, and although all right for adults, had nothing to offer young children and teenagers.

Punnett's town itself, was situated on one road and contained a few houses, a butcher, a bakery, general store, an old Victorian school and the Barley Mow public house. This village is where my mother and auntie were born and grew up, that was until my grandfather, the licensee of the pub, decided enough was enough of being a landlord and built a bungalow in the next village. My auntie still lived in the village with her husband on a farm, which is where we arrived late on the Tuesday evening.

Two weeks had passed since moving in with my auntie and uncle and I tried desperately to settle in with my surroundings and spent time getting to know the animals and helping to collect the chicken's eggs. My auntie would milk the cows, Buttercup and Daisy, and then show me how to make butter from it, but none of it was what I wanted and nothing compensated for the lonely unhappiness I felt.

In the end, the inevitable arrived, time to start a new school. On the first day of school, for some reason Mum did not take me, but my cousin Norma did instead. We'd reached the black railings that guarded the school perimeter. I was scared and didn't want to walk through the big heavy gates.

Norma held my hand tight and told me it would be alright, that I would soon make friends with the other children. I was so unsure as I looked at the old building. It was so dirty and dismal looking, I thought I'd never come out alive, or they would keep me in there and not let me leave, or worst still my Mum would have gone away when I came out. Eventually Norma persuaded me to go in, promising everything would be ok.

By dinnertime my fear had abated somewhat and after eating, all the children rushed out to play in the school yard. I followed and stood by the wall watching the boys and girls running around laughing and playing together. I really wanted to join in and I waited all dinnertime for someone to ask me, but no one did.

Days went by, but I still felt isolated by the other children's silence towards me, and huddled myself in the furthest corner of the school yard and cried. One day I heard a teacher's voice asking me what was the matter. Until then, I hadn't realised the bell had gone and all the children had gone inside. I tried to explain in an upset gibberish voice, that none of the other children liked me, they didn't speak to me I felt so unhappy, and I wanted to go home, to my real home.

A few days later, while we were at lunch, to my surprise I was asked if I would like to play after we had eaten. I'd noticed these children before, but they never played with anyone else. I looked up and answered with a very quiet yes please. At last, I'd made two friends and after that day school didn't seem so bad.

Samantha and Jack were brother and sister and lived at a house in the lane that was opposite the Barley Mow. The other children were still not talking to me, but somehow now it didn't matter. Each morning whoever got to school first, would wait for the other to arrive, and whether we were in class, at dinner, or at play we became inseparable. One day I couldn't wait to tell Mum I'd been invited to Sam and Jack's for tea and asked if I could go. She had agreed until my auntie told her where and how they lived. She told Mum they were dirty tinkers and they couldn't be trusted and that I shouldn't mix with them. That night I went to bed very upset and lonely again, I wondered how I was going to tell them I couldn't go for tea, and would they fallout with me? The next morning my eyes still red from crying, I begged Mum to let me go. She finally agreed to think about it and would let me know when she picked me up later. I told Sam and Jack that I wouldn't know until Mum came to collect me after school if I could go for tea, but all day it worried me. Little did I know

Mum had gone to see Mr and Mrs Carter to check up on them for herself. Mum felt sure the family were Romanies and not tinkers, and she decided I could go to tea, seeing no reason why I should not be friends with Sam and Jack. I was so relieved, and I probably didn't realise at the time that Mum was fighting my corner.

Auntie on the other hand made her feelings well known. She disliked the thought of any of her family associating with those kinds of people, to her they were the lowest of the low and she refused for weeks to allow Sam and Jack anywhere on the farm.

Sometime after we arrived at the farm Mum bought a seven-berth caravan and had it placed in the top field behind the battery shed. This allowed auntie to have her house back and Mum and me to have our own place and settle into some sort of routine.

Life continued, but I hadn't seen my Dad and was really missing him. Whenever I asked Mum about him, she told me he would come down when he had rented out the house and shop, but when I asked how long that would be, she never really answered me because she was either too busy or too tired to discuss it. She didn't seem to appreciate how much I missed Dad, and how desperate I was to see him. On two occasions I received a letter from Dad saying that he hadn't forgotten me and he still loved me and looked forward to seeing me. In a way that made it harder as I couldn't understand why he didn't come down and join us at the caravan.

Within days of moving to Punnett's town, Mrs Parrott, the head of the Area Health Visitors board, offered Mum a job as a home help. As this was in and around the Punnett's town area it was convenient for Mum to walk to work, as she couldn't drive. Six months on Mrs Parrott offered Mum another job which would better suit her experience and training. In her teens, Mum had gained considerable nursing knowledge and experience at the mental hospital but had never taken examinations to qualify as a nurse. The position Mrs Parrott had offered her was one of general household duties and basic nursing skills, which included giving an insulin injection twice a day. This would be a one-to-one full time job, the only problem was it was ten miles away in Cross in Hand. This was a small village close to Punnett's town, but there was no direct bus service between the villages, so this meant we had to move to Cross in Hand.

Cross In Hand was where my Granddad had built his bungalow and although he had passed away some years ago, my gran was still very much alive. Mum had made her decision to accept the job and move in with gran, taking me with her. Again, I was the last person to be told but then again, I was only a child and perhaps my thoughts on the matter or how the move may affect me was not considered important enough to be taken into consideration. I didn't know my Gran that well and had only seen her a few times, but the times I had seen her, I felt a warmth towards her and an incredible sense of unconditional love. But despite my feeling towards my Gran, I suddenly felt lost all over again. I did not want to move, even to Grans. It had taken me months to become half settled and make new friends and I didn't want to go through it all again. I wanted to stay with auntie even though she did frighten me. In a way it seemed a lessor torment than starting another school.

Saturday came and all our bags once more were packed and ready to go. I'd already said goodbye to

Sam and Jack the day before and was now doing my rounds with the animals. First came the chickens and then Buttercup and Daisy and finally the pig and her piglets. I loved the pigs most of all, the way they rolled around and snorted at feeding time made me laugh. I tried so hard to hide when it was time to go, but Mum found me. I begged not to go, I pleaded with auntie to let me stay, but she simply said "See you soon" and walked into the house and shut the door behind her. Mum shouted at me to get into the taxi; I tried to run away but she caught me and pushed me through the door and made me sit in the back seat. I had no choice other than to accept I had to go with her.

My Gran was a lovely person, she tried so hard to make me happy. She would play games with me, and talk to me about all sorts of things, giving me the time and attention Mum did not, but I still felt I'd taken a step backwards from being settled at the farm and my new school, to suddenly not being settled at all. I know I was in a lovely house, had food in my tummy and clothes to wear. I had a gran who loved me and really cared, but somehow, I seemed to have lost my Mum. Yes, she was there in person but not once in six months had she reassured me or given me a kiss or cuddle. I felt so lonely, and as a child I could not understand why I had this deep feeling of sadness all the time. With no-one to confide in, my confusion deepened and manifested itself by developing a mistrust of everyone, but especially my Mum, the very person I should have felt safe with.

I had started at a new school in Cross in Hand and was again finding it very difficult to settle. This time it had taken a great deal longer to make a friend but when

I eventually did, I found the friendship did not extend beyond school hours. At the end of each day, we went our own way, and I had no friends out of school. I missed Sam and Jack, and none of my friends at the new school seemed to understand me as they had, so the friendships never developed other than school mates.

I was going through a difficult time, and I needed to spend time with my Mum. I wanted her to be how she used to be, like a Mum again, but unfortunately with her new job she almost ignored me. Every weekend she still had to work either Saturday or Sunday which meant even less time with her. One day I asked her if I could go with her to work, I promised to be good, and I'd help if I could. Surprisingly Mum agreed, providing Mrs Scothmere did not object, which she didn't. Mrs Scothmere lived on her own in a cottage where she had lived most of her life. She was no longer as mobile as she used to be, and needed help with everyday chores, and as she did not have any family living locally, Mum was employed to provide the care she needed. She was a lovely elderly lady, and we would sit and talk, play games and share time together. Most importantly, she brought a smile to my face. At the end of the day, she would give me a hug before we left. In the end I went with Mum, not to be with my Mum, but to spend time with an old lady who was treating me like a daughter, because my Mum certainly wasn't. I will always remember her as someone who showed me kindness, and we both shared a companionship which we valued.

On week days, after school I'd play on my own at the back of the bungalow. The garden stretched about two hundred yards until you came to the woods, also owned by Gran, but I never walked into them more than a few feet. On the edge of the woods, over the style ran a stream with a piece of wood across it to form a bridge; gran told me granddad had placed it there years ago so she could cross the stream without getting her feet wet! The stream was no more than a foot deep, gently meandering and covering the tiny stones. I'd sit there for hours watching the water gently going on its way, not really understanding what I was thinking or even what I was doing there. Mum would very rarely come and join me, but on many occasions, gran would bring a drink and a biscuit and come and sit with me. She would chat about everything and nothing but would always end up asking me why I didn't have a friend around to play. Each time I couldn't answer her because I didn't know, and I couldn't explain how I was feeling; I could not put into words the loneliness and isolation I felt, and how I missed the love of my Mum. Gran was very perceptive, and I know she tried to make up for my lack of friends, but at the end of the day she was my Gran not my playmate.

The months carried on and nothing really changed except the time of the year. In February I received a birthday card from Dad. I was now six and it seemed a lifetime since I'd seen him. I loved my Dad very much and it was awful not having him around. I desperately wanted to be part of a loving family, with both my Mum and Dad, all living together.

It wasn't long after my birthday that Mrs Parrot offered Mum another job, this one didn't include her nursing skills but one of just housekeeping.

Nationally, each area health authority had a department which dealt with bereaved widowers with children. The aim was to employ women in each authority to become a housekeeper for the bereaved father and child for a six-month period. In this time, it was thought the grieving process would have eased, and the widower would have learnt new skills to enable him to cope with family life without his wife. The authorities also decided to set up a register of relief housekeepers. This was women who were prepared to travel throughout the country and provide emergency support wherever it was needed.

The position offered to Mum was one of living in housekeeper to a man who had recently lost his wife. Again, Mum made the decision to accept the job without even explaining to me what was happening, and this time it wasn't anywhere near my Gran or auntie but miles away in Leighton Buzzard. Within a week, our bags were packed, arrangements had been finalised and we were on our way. This time I didn't try to hide, beg to stay or even cry, I just accepted we were going and there was nothing I could do about it. I wasn't asked how I felt or what I thought, so I said nothing just accepting the situation. Although I hadn't formed any close friends at school, I had grown close to Gran, and leaving her was another wrench I found difficult to cope with, and there was the dread of starting at yet another new school.

We arrived in Leighton Buzzard in the early afternoon. The train station wasn't that busy and Mum found a taxi quite easily. While making its way to the address Mum had given the taxi driver, I notice there weren't any fields or open spaces, no animals or birds, in fact nothing but houses and shops. I had instantly taken a dislike to the place, it was ugly, with big buildings and far too much noise. For the first time in my life, I felt scared as this all seemed like a foreign place to me with no familiar landmarks. I wanted to run and get away from this place that seemed so alien to me. I don't know where I thought I would go, but I just wanted to get as far away as I could. Gran's smiling face came into my mind, and I so wanted a hug from her, but she wasn't here. I looked across at Mum and went to take her hand, but she ignored me as she leant forward to speak to the driver.

A few minutes later we pulled up outside a house. It was a traditional style suburban house and looked no different from all the others in the street, except this one was to be my new home. Mr. Roberts was there to greet us and introduce us to his son. They both seemed very nice and showed us to our room before offering us refreshments.

The following day, with breakfast over, I left Mum talking to Mr. Roberts while I went upstairs to find the ragdoll my gran had given me. The bedroom was quite large, with a double bed, a wardrobe and dressing table and a rather moth-eaten chair in one corner. The bed had pink flannelette sheets with matching pillow cases and was covered by an old off-white eiderdown.

I found my ragdoll and managed to climb up onto the bed and sit on the edge. From here I could see out of the window and down onto the driveway that led up to the house. I could still hear Mum and Mr. Roberts talking in the kitchen. Suddenly Matthew, who was about 10 years old, unannounced came into the room and closed the door behind him. Still sitting on the bed holding my ragdoll, he came close to me pointing his finger and told me he hated me and my Mum being there and not to go into his room; I wasn't to touch any of his things and if I told my Mum what he had said I would be "dead meat".

After he left the room, I huddled on the bed cuddling my ragdoll tightly. I started crying like I had never cried before. I wondered why Mum had brought me to such a horrible place. I felt so miserable, alone, and unloved. I started to question why we had to keep moving, why did I have to keep going to a new school, why couldn't I have stayed with Gran. I hated Mum for putting me through all this; why couldn't she see I needed to be loved and to have some stability in my life. I also needed my Dad; I missed him so much as he was the one person I knew I could talk to and he would understand how I felt. I wanted to play with other children but now I was too frightened to make new friends as I knew I would leave them when we moved on. All I wanted was to feel safe and loved by my Mum.

The following months were not happy; with continued verbal abuse from Matthew and no real friends at school, I became lonelier and increasingly introvert. I spent most of my time alone in the bedroom with only my ragdoll for company. My imagination ran wild, and I regularly made-up games about a happy little girl, playing with her friends, having fun without a care in the world. And then of course I would come back to reality as I was called for tea, and my imaginary friends would melt away leaving me alone once more.

While we were at Leighton Buzzard, I was shocked to hear about the death of my Gran, but it meant our time at Leighton Buzzard was interrupted for a day or so for us to return to Sussex. Gran died as result of her injuries caused by falling down three flights of steps.

I never really understood what had happened, as she always seemed quite fit and not the sort of person to just fall down some stairs. But, like everything else, no-one actually explained to me what had happened. Gan had been laid out in the front room of the bungalow, as was the tradition in those days, and while Mum and auntie were deliberating whether it was healthy for me to see her or not, I slipped in unnoticed. I hadn't seen anyone dead before and possibly I didn't really understand the situation, but I wasn't frightened, I just felt a deep sadness.

After a couple of days, we returned to Leighton Buzzard to complete Mum's six month assignment, after which we were on the move again, this time to High Wycombe and yet another six months of turmoil, new school, new home and only a ragdoll to confide in. I was now seven and a half years old and, on the move, yet again. As the train pulled out of the station I looked out of the window and saw derelict railway sidings and tall dirty buildings. I was suddenly aware of my Mum's voice, and it was only when I heard the word caravan that brought me out of my trance. Had I heard the word caravan, could I believe what she was saying, we were going back to the farm, back to the caravan, which I now felt was my safe place.

CHAPTER THREE

Back on the farm nothing changed, it was almost as though time had stood still. Daisy and Buttercup were still there, also the pigs, although different ones by now but just like the others they snorted and played in their styes. The chickens and ducks were still wandering around the yard pecking intermittently for grit. Probably the thing that overwhelmed me the most was the open fields. I ran to the gate and climbed over, rushing halfway down the field, and then stopping. I smelt the breeze as is it curled around my face and into my hair, it was wonderful, it felt so good.

While allowing my senses to enjoy this pleasure, I heard my name being called by someone who sounded familiar, but it wasn't a voice that I readily recognised as it belonged to a man. I was too far away to see who it was so thought I'd better start walking back. As I drew closer to the figure standing by the gate my heart started to beat almost out of control. It was my Dad; I could now see him clearly. I ran as fast as my little legs would carry me but tripped and fell over. I tried quickly to get up, but it didn't matter, Dad was already picking me up and hugging me. It felt so good to have his arms around me, and I felt the warmth and comfort I had so missed while we had been separated. I thought perhaps now everything would be alright.

The following twelve months were rather uneventful. I started back at Punnett's town school and met up with Sam and Jack again. For a while our friendship was difficult to rekindle but was worth it in the end and we were soon firm friends again. My Dad in the meantime was trying to catch up for lost time, but somehow, he had changed or so I thought. I loved him with a passion, he was my Dad, but he had become a stranger to me, it wasn't his fault, it wasn't mine either, but sadly we had grown apart during the long period of separation. I suppose he expected me to need him, but I had become independent, so if anyone had changed it was me.

The year was now 1964 and we had been living in the caravan for the past twelve months. As usual I was up before Mum and Dad to fetch the bread and milk from the farmhouse. Why Mum sent me was beyond me. The milk was safe but the bread was something else! It was a Tin loaf that always smelt wonderful, and unfortunately the temptation was always too great, by the time I got back to the caravan it looked like mice had been gnawing their way through it. One particular morning, I shouted to Mum I was off to fetch the bread and milk, and I would be back in a few minutes. I opened the caravan door and taking no notice that it needed an extra shove, only to find myself not walking down the steps but stepping into a massive snow drift. Hearing my alarm call, and after some searching Mum finally found me, very cold and wet, looking like a drowned rat almost completely engulfed in snow. This was the first time I could ever remember Mum really taking any notice of me and the first time we had ever laughed together. She dried me off, changed my clothes and decided it was safer for her to get the bread that morning instead.

A few weeks after the snow blizzard the weather broke and returned to normal for the time of year, by which time it was discovered that the caravan had sustained some serious damage. I didn't really understand the ins and outs of what was wrong but whatever it was, it resulted in the caravan being sold.

This of course created a problem as to where to live. We couldn't stay with auntie because her daughter Norma lived there with her husband, and they had just had a baby who occupied the spare room. In the end it was decided that Dad would return home to Redditch and try to terminate the tenancy agreement, while Mum and I moved back to Cross in Hand. Gran's bungalow had been sold so we couldn't go there, but eventually moved in with a friend of Mums from years ago. I returned to Cross in Hand school and became withdrawn and isolated, having again lost my friends from Punnett's town.

Approximately twelve months after Dad had returned home Mum and I also returned to Redditch, although by this time Dad had closed the shop. Home - I wasn't sure that's what it was anymore. I know it had been home years ago, but it felt strange and unfamiliar to me. I had a distant memory of it, but it may as well have been any one of the many places I'd been in during recent years. Although this really was home, I had more empathy with the farm, which now felt more like home than Redditch did.

I started lessons at my original school and twelve months later I took my eleven plus examination. The educational system hadn't failed me, but my home circumstances had and I failed miserably. I managed to scrape through to attend secondary school, but goodness knows how. Perhaps at the time they didn't have special schools as I could hardly write, I couldn't spell and figures, well a simple addition confused me. The friends I had made when I first started at the school had long since moved on to new friendships which I was not part of.

By now Mum was working in a factory and she had undergone a complete character change; nothing was too much trouble and she suddenly started to show me affection. She would talk to me and constantly be concerned about my welfare. Although this was good I didn't know how to deal with it, as I wasn't used to this amount of attention, however I slowly became accustomed to it and for once, I felt less isolated and started to trust that Mum was now thinking of me and how I was feeling. I still didn't have any friends, not because I didn't want friends, I certainly did, but I didn't know how to start to make friendships. I was confused about everything, and in particular Mum's new attention towards me, which soon became so obsessive and over powering I started to resent it. This was strange because for so many years I had yearned her attention, but it had now become suffocating.

The next few years passed without any real traumas, and as a family we settled into a routine. The dining room / shop had been converted into a bedsit and blocked from the remainder of the house. This area was ultimately rented out to a man who worked with Mum at the factory. Apparently, he had moved to Redditch and was living in digs that didn't really suit him and the bedsit was ideal. For a man with only a few personal effects I suppose it wasn't bad. The main room was small but big enough for a single bed, a chair, a small table and a chest of drawers. The existing door and window let light into the room, but the door was not used, and entrance to the bedsit was via a door at the back onto the yard. The room at the back was much smaller but managed to contain a sink, work surface with a baby belling cooker standing on the top, with a small free-standing fridge on the floor just underneath. The door in the corner gave entrance to the rear yard and garden and allowed Matthew freedom to come and go without disturbing us.

Within a few months Matthew settled in and with Mum's agreement, he had taken charge of the garden because Dad could no longer manage it. Dad was ten years older than Mum and was now fifty-one. Although most people that age are quite fit and well, Dad wasn't. He had never fully recovered totally from T.B. meningitis, it left him partly deaf and suffering from vertigo. If that wasn't enough, he repeatedly suffered from bouts of bronchitis, and I can't remember a time when he didn't cough.

I was about thirteen and had completed the first two years at secondary school. I was still lonely because I hadn't made any friends to speak about and I became even more introverted. Although to some degree I had formed a sort of friendship with Matthew, it wasn't like having friends of my own age. In a sense I couldn't understand why Dad was ill and Matthew wasn't, it seemed so unfair. In the end he became like a second Dad to me, in as much he would talk to me and showed me how to do different things in the garden. Mum was being more like I expected a Mum to be, but I felt smothered by her attention, I was so used to being ignored by her. However, in a mixed-up way I started to feel I was part of a normal family. Mum had told me that it didn't matter that I didn't have any friends because all I would ever need was her. She said at the end of the day friends end up hurting you, which your mother will never do, and to always remember, your mother will be the best friend you'll ever have, and never let you down. All this seemed a bit ironic, considering Mum's total lack of consideration for me for so many years.

Several months after starting my third year at school, I was involved in a disturbance, in fact I was instigator. I wanted it to blow up into a full-blown fight, but it never got that far. A girl in the same year as me had for some months picked on younger pupils. She started off belittling them in front of their friends, and progressively increased her bullying by pulling their hair and hitting them. When I saw her doing this, it instantly brought back memories of my time in Leighton Buzzard and I knew exactly how these girls must have been feeling, and I didn't want them to suffer as I had.

On the day I got involved, she had started to pick on yet another girl, she was like that, she spent a few weeks picking on one, then started on another. But this particular day I decided enough was enough and she had to be stopped. It didn't occur to me that I hadn't any friends to back me up, I was so angry, although, I must admit it did feel slightly daunting. At dinner time I purposely sat on the table she was sitting at. I told her what I thought of her, and that she should pick on someone her own size and I will be waiting in the playground. When she finally came out, as promised

I was there waiting for her. I started to goad her, until in the end I slapped her across the face hoping she would retaliate and it would instigate a fight, but she didn't react. I pushed her and taunted her into responding, I wanted her to receive some of her own medicine, but she still wouldn't take up the challenge. She probably knew I was physically stronger than her, and so she resorted to verbal abuse and spitefully told me my Dad was not my real Dad, and everyone knew other than me before walking away leaving me in a state of confusion.

For weeks I questioned whether the information Sandra had given me was true or whether she made it up, just to hurt me. I didn't want to believe her and tried to push it to the back of my mind, but it wouldn't go away, it just kept rearing its ugly head all the time. My Dad was lovely and I loved him to bits and I could never imagine having any other Dad. I really didn't know what to believe anymore and whether I really wanted to know the truth. In the end the torment of watching Dad and always wondering if what Sandra had said was true became an obsession. Finally, I made the decision, I had to know the truth once and for all and so decided to ask Mum.

One night after Dad had gone to bed, I told Mum what Sandra had said, and I asked her if it was true. For once Mum was honest with me and said, yes, it was true that my Dad wasn't my biological father, and she wished I hadn't found out in the way I had. She had hoped that I would have been older when she told me, which would have made it easier for me to understand, but she would try to explain it to me. She started by telling me that Phillip was the name of my biological father, and as far as she knew his parents, my grandparents, were still alive and lived not far away in Ham Green. She hesitated at this point and told me there was not a simple explanation, but she would try her best to make me understand, although she would have to start a long time before I was born.

Mum told me at the age of twenty-one she still lived with her parents in Sussex but unfortunately the Second World War had broken out and it became extremely difficult to find work. As it was a rural area, she could have worked on the land but she didn't want to. The only other option she had, was to come up north and decided to move to Coventry. However, before she reached Coventry the train was diverted due to an air raid, and it started to make its way towards Birmingham. This destination wasn't to be met either due to damage caused to the track, and eventually stopped at Redditch. By this time, she was tired and hungry and found a bed and breakfast for the night, deciding to sort something out the next day.

The following day instead of travelling on to Coventry she looked for work in Redditch. The landlady had told her that a local factory, Terry Springs, was looking for people and the rates of pay weren't too bad. She managed to get a job there and continued to board with the same woman, who eventually became a great friend. The weeks and months passed and she settled into life in Redditch, making friends with her work colleagues. One night as a dare, she went out on a blind date with one of her friends and her boyfriend. During the evening, she met a tall, dark haired handsome man dressed in his Sunday best who all the girls fancied, and apparently he was known as the catch of Redditch. They started going out together and got engaged and then married three years later. Before the marriage, Dad still lived with his parents, who were thinking of moving house, so when they finally got married, his parents moved out and Mum and Dad moved in. The house was a wedding present from Mum's parents.

Mum explained, after a few years she became pregnant with Dad's child but because of complications the baby was stillborn. She had been rushed into the Women's Hospital in Birmingham and she had nearly lost her life. The doctors explained the baby had probably died some time ago, and although it had a spinal cord, it hadn't a vertebra and the back of the skull had not formed properly.

Mum tried to explain the reason for the malformation of the foetus wasn't through her but was Dad's fault because he wasn't a proper man. She told me he couldn't achieve and hold an erection for any length of time. She asked me if I understood and when I said yes, she continued to say, in those days sex wasn't talked about with your parents and therefore she didn't know what to expect. So, when she married, she thought half an erection was normal. After a few more years, Dad couldn't manage an erection at all and Mum had resigned herself to the fact that the physical side of the marriage was over, and so was the chance of her ever getting pregnant again.

Sometime later Mum and Dad decided take in a lodger, which would help with the bills. Within the space of a couple of weeks Phillip was settling in, and they thought they'd made the right choice.

However, approximately twelve months later Dad became ill. After numerous tests he was taken into East Birmingham isolation hospital. He was extremely ill, and the doctors didn't expect him to make it through the night, but he did. A week later and after more tests they discovered that he was suffering not just with meningitis but TB meningitis. The doctors had informed Mum the survival rate from this illness was very low indeed and to expect a phone call at any minute. The Doctor also recommended that anyone in the household should be screened every month by X-ray, and whatever the outcome with Dad, screening should continue for a period of eighteen months. Screening started for Mum and Philip, and Dad started his treatment. All Mum and Phillip had to do was stand in front of an X-ray machine, but Dad's treatment was far more complicated and sometimes very painful. At the time this country did not have a cure for this illness and relied on an untrialled drug from the States called streptomycin. There was no other way of giving this treatment other than by a lumbar puncture twice a day. Two or three months into the treatment, Dad hadn't become any worse but neither had he improved, the doctors were still of the opinion that Dad wouldn't make it, and that the inevitable would happen.

Mum said she didn't know what to believe or how she felt. She told me one day she had been out from eight in the morning until six at night, and when she got home she felt exhausted and started crying in front of Philip. Before she realised Phillip was holding her in his arms and while trying to comfort her, they kissed. She knew it was wrong, but it had been such a long time since anyone had taken any notice of her, or she'd had any close physical contact with a man. She said it felt wonderful, and although she felt guilty, found she couldn't and did not want to stop. She said for years she hadn't loved Dad as a wife, but more as a sister. And so, an affair began between Mum and Philip. She thought from what the doctors told her, that Dad wouldn't survive to know about the affair. Phillip told her when the time was right, he wanted to marry her. But when Mum became pregnant by Phillip, she realised the desire for a child was far greater than her feelings for him and she certainly did not want to marry him.

After Mum had finished telling me the truth about my biological father, she asked if I had any questions, but to be honest, it was taking me time to process all of this and try to understand what she was telling me. It was quite a story and I think Mum had expected me to feel sorry for her and to a certain extent I did, but the person I felt the most pain and hurt for was my Dad. He didn't deserve what Mum and Phillip had done to him, least of all to realise it had happened when he had been in hospital fighting for his life.

For weeks I puzzled over Mum's story and, as children do, I became inquisitive, not really understanding the full implications of it all. I wondered what Philip looked like and what type of person he was, and I realised I had to find out. I broached the subject with Mum and asked if she thought it would be possible for me to meet him. After asking me if it was truly what I wanted, she said she would think about it. Mum left it for a few weeks, I suppose to see if I would ask again, which of course I did. Finally, it was arranged that I would go to see my Gran and Granddad first. I remember it as if it was yesterday. Mum wouldn't come with me; she dropped me at the gate and waited in the car. I must admit, I was apprehensive and a little scared to tell the truth. The house was in the country and looked quite old with a path leading to the front door. After shutting the gate behind me, and as I started to walk along the path I wondered if it was such a good idea; I was about to meet two people I'd never seen before, never met and it felt really strange.

I knocked the door and before I had time to run, the door was answered. An old, tall, thin man looked down at me with a smile and said "Hello you must be Shane, come on in and meet your Gran".

Grandma was just the opposite to Granddad; she was quite a large woman and very rarely smiled but had a wicked sense of humour. The hour I spent with them passed quickly, and although we did not talk about anything in particular, I felt a certain closeness to them and comfortable in their company. When I left both Grandad and Grandma gave me a hug and said how pleased they were to have met me at last. Back in the car, Mum asked me how I had got on, but this was mine, and I did not want to share it with anyone, so I just said "yes, it was good thanks." Although Mum quizzed me for more information, I kept my answers to her questions short, not giving anything away.

Through meeting my grandparents, they arranged for me to meet with Philip, and although a few weeks passed before I heard from them, eventually a time and place for us to meet was agreed. Mum came with me to the first meeting. There were no emotional hugs or declarations of parental love. In fact, Mum and Philip did most of the talking with me offering the occasional "yes" or "no" to various questions. It was the strangest experience I had ever encountered and I cannot even begin to explain all the different emotions I felt that day.

I was still a child and had only ever known one Dad, so to be confronted with this situation was over whelming and I never gave any thought to what this may be doing to Dad.

Many more meetings followed and with each one I learnt something new. He was an extremely tall dark-haired man of medium build. He had been married but was now divorced and he told me I had two half-brothers and two half-sisters who lived in Nottingham. We subsequently met on two occasions, but no bonding or friendship ever materialised. Each I time I met him I still couldn't come to terms with the fact that he was my biological father. I started to become concerned because I really did not have any strong feelings towards him, although my Mum thought I should have. He was a stranger to me, and it didn't matter how many times I met him I knew nothing would change that. Of course, I had no idea what renewing this friendship with Philip would have on Mum, after all they had been very close at one time.

Within a couple of months of my first meeting with Philip, Dad went to Sussex for a week, goodness knows what for and to this day I really cannot believe it was his idea to go. Whilst Dad was away, to my surprise Philip moved back into the house for the week. I can't remember why or even what happened, but I remember I didn't want him there. I felt Philip was nothing to do with me, and despite a biological connection, I certainly did not see him as a father figure, and yet Mum seemed to try to push me to accept him. As far as I was concerned, I had one Dad, and he was in Sussex. Philip moved out the day before my Dad returned home. From that day on, I did not see Philip again. It seemed to me he had abused my Dad's trust for a second time and as far as I was concerned Mum was no better.

Probably for the first time I realised just how much I really did love my Dad and I felt it was unfair that Mum and Philip had cheated on him yet again. Dad never knew Phillip had stayed with us the week he was in Sussex; I was told never to tell him, and I never did. But I suspect he knew something was going on because Mum had told Dad that I had met Philip and maybe that is why he went to Sussex. I remember saying to Dad I was sorry for going to meet Philip, but I just wanted to know what he was like. I also said that I really did not like him and there was only one Dad for me. I remember looking at my Dad and telling him that I loved him, and I wouldn't hurt him again or allow others to hurt him. I respected my Dad far too much and from that day we re-captured the bond we had lost years ago while we were separated.

The subject of Philip never came up again but it remained at the forefront of everyone's mind. For me it was the confusion of a biological father I neither knew nor particularly liked; for Mum it was, all be it for a short period, renewing a lost friendship and for Dad it brought back the fact he had not been able to father a child of his own. It was tough going for a while, but we got through it, other than Dad who seemed to have lost some of his contentment. He had taken a turn for the worst and whether it was a coincidence I didn't know, but he became quite ill. The doctors at first thought he may be suffering from a severe chest infection, but a few weeks later he deteriorated and was admitted to the Queen Elizabeth Hospital in Birmingham. Some weeks passed and the surgeons eventually decided to undertake an exploratory operation, during which they discovered that he had cancer. He underwent further examinations, and to the best of the surgeon's knowledge, he had removed all the malignant growth.

Dad stayed in hospital for six weeks with Mum visiting him each evening after work, getting home about ten pm. It was easier now because Mum had learnt to drive, although she hated driving in Birmingham. I would go with her sometimes, but this meant a bit of a rush because I would come home from school, make a flask of coffee and sandwiches to take with us. By the time I'd washed and changed, Mum would be arriving home from work just in time for a cup of tea, and we'd be off. The times I didn't go, I'd do some housework, light the fire and start the tea for when Mum came home, but she was often too tired to eat and just wanted to go to bed.

Matthew was trying his best to help, and Mum was spending a great deal of time with him. I suppose she was worried about Dad and wanted someone to talk to, an adult rather than a child. The only trouble was this meant the person I needed a hug and reassurance from was never around. I recall one night in particular, I hadn't gone to the hospital because of how it had upset me the previous night. Dad had been in considerable pain from the drainage tubes, and I could not cope seeing him like it again. Mum came back as usual at about ten pm. I had made the fire, tidied up and managed to do all the washing, which at that time was done by hand as we didn't have a washing machine. I made a cup of tea the minute she came in and told her I had prepared the dinner, and it wouldn't be above

10 minutes. I asked how Dad was and did he appear any better? Mum told me he wasn't too bad, and not to worry, and immediately went to see Matthew. I sat there for an hour or more waiting for Mum to come back, but I finally went to bed with the dinner I had prepared now inedible.

Tucked up in bed, I tried to understand why Mum would rather spend time with Matthew than me, but I couldn't. I thought of how often she would go around there and that she'd had an affair with Philip the last time Dad was in hospital. Surely she couldn't be having an affair with Matthew. Was it following the same pattern as before? I cried into my pillow, feeling so sad for my Dad who knew nothing of what may be happening, and thought of how he was being betrayed again by Mum.

During the time Dad was in hospital Mum wasn't very forthcoming about his condition, she left me in the dark, never discussing what the doctors were saying about his condition. Although I was still only thirteen, I wasn't an immature child who didn't understand the severity of the situation. Mum knew how much I loved my Dad and it was awful not being able to share my fears with her. She reverted to being the person who didn't show me any love or even think about me. Her life revolved around the hospital, work and visiting Matthew every spare minute she had. Once again, I felt ignored by Mum and detached from her, with her showing me no affection or consideration.

One day, I remember all too well an experience that was to change my life and destroy my faith in human nature and my self-esteem. Mun had gone to the hospital and as usual I stayed at home. We had already agreed that I would make cauliflower cheese for tea, and Mum had asked me to cook enough for Matthew because he had been very good to her, and it would be nice to do some food for him.

After I had cooked the tea, and worrying whether I had asked Mum to tell Dad that I loved him, I took a plate of piping hot cauliflower cheese to Matthew. He answered the door with his usual smile and jolly nature. I explained that Mum had asked me to cook extra and hoped he enjoyed it. I turned towards the door to leave, but he stopped me asking, was I alright as he knew how I must be feeling about my Dad. He told me not to worry too much because he would be fine and would be home in no time. I suppose that was all it took. A few kind words from Matthew and I broke down and sobbed. Matthew asked me what I feared, and I told him I didn't want my Dad to die. Matthew put his arms around me and hugged me; this made me cry even more. Why was someone that wasn't a member of my family showing me more affection than my Mum was? In the end, I didn't know why I was crying, whether it was for my Dad, my Mum's indifference or because I felt so lonely.

I explained to Matthew that I felt no one loved me anymore except my Dad, and I was afraid he was going to die. Matthew looked me straight in the eye and told me that, of course Dad wasn't going to die, and as for Mum, of course, she loved me. He also told me that he loved me too and that you don't have to be related to someone to love them. This confused me, and I asked him what he meant. He didn't answer me but gave me a big warm hug, it felt so good especially as I was not having any comforting hugs from Mum. After a minute or two, I told Matthew that I would be alright and I should get back, but he wouldn't let me go. I tried to pull away because I felt smothered, and felt as though I couldn't breathe, and I began to feel slightly apprehensive. He took hold of my hand and pushed it into his groin. I could feel what was obviously his penis. It was long and hard and felt as if at any minute it would burst through his trousers. I was so shocked; I told him to stop it and tried to pull away but he kissed me on the mouth. I fought as hard as possible and finally he pulled away. He told me this was how he loved me, and he wouldn't hurt me but I was very special to him.

As he eased his grip on me, I took my chance and ran to the door, pushed the handle down, but nothing happened. I tried again with all my might, but I realised he had locked it. Mortified, I begged him to unlock it; I just wanted my Dad. Matthew came towards me; I could see the bulge in his trousers where he had placed my hand only minutes ago. I begged and screamed at him to let me go, but he repeatedly said that he loved me. I shouted at him to open the door, and if he didn't, I would tell Mum. He just laughed and said Mum wouldn't believe me because half the time it's as if I don't exist to her. Smiling at me, he unlocked the door but told me if I were to tell Mum, it would be worse for me next time. I ran into the house locking the door behind me and went to my room.

I huddled on the bed, still and emotionless, not really understanding what had just happened. But I did know Matthew had acted inappropriately, and that he was a grown man and I was only a child and there is no way he should have done what he did, or made me feel like this. I don't know how long I stayed on my bed, but a sudden knocking at the back door brought a sense of panic, like an electric shock. The door was knocked again, and I heard Matthew calling me. I sat bolt-upright on the bed, struggling to remember whether I had locked the back door, fear running through my veins at what he might do if he got into the house. Then I heard a thud downstairs and thinking Matthew must be in the house I hid under the bed clothes, but then I heard Mum's voice; she must have just arrived home and I breathed a sigh of relief. She asked Matthew if he was alright, and I heard him say he had come round to thank me for the wonderful tea. Mum called me to come down stairs because Matthew wanted to see me. I didn't know what to say, I didn't want to go down and face him, so I quickly replied, "I'm undressed". Pacified, I could hear Mum talking to Matthew. I suddenly thought Mum would wonder why I was still dressed, so I quickly changed into my pyjamas just in case she came up to see me.

Matthew went home about half an hour later, and Mum called me to come down. I had so hoped she would come upstairs to find out if I was alright, and I would be able to tell her what had occurred. But instead, I went down and acted as if nothing had happened. I asked how Dad was and she told me he was not too bad, and could come home in about two weeks. I should have been overjoyed at this news, and any other time I would have been, but I couldn't feel excited as all I could think about was Matthew and what he had done to me. I could not understand what he had said, only that he made me feel sick and dirty. I desperately wanted to tell Mum and anguished over whether I should, but Matthew was probably right, considering how Mum treated me, she wouldn't believe me. I felt I had no choice but to keep out of Matthews's way and say nothing.

Two weeks had passed since the incident with Matthew, and I still had a sickening unrest in my stomach and couldn't understand why he had treated me in that way. During the months Matthew had lived next door, I'd come to respect him as a friend who would always be there but now I felt hurt and confused by his actions. The friendship and respect had gone, and all I could do was keep away, but I also missed him as a friend which added to my confusion. In the meantime, Dad had been discharged from hospital, but he didn't seem any better. One night after Dad had gone to bed and Mum had eventually returned from Matthews; I asked her if Dad was alright. I was most surprised when she offered to make me a cup of tea, and to sit down and talk to me. When the tea was made, Mum sat down in the chair furthest away from me and began to explain what was wrong with Dad and what the surgeons had done. She wasn't telling me anything I hadn't already worked out for myself. I couldn't help but feel hurt and wondered why after such a long time, she had decided to talk to me now when I had needed her to talk to and reassure me when Dad was in hospital. I suppose this sudden concern towards me didn't wash because I didn't know where I stood with her. One minute she would be obsessed with me, and the next, not care how I was. She was still talking to me, but I was only half listening until I heard her say that Dad had only six weeks to live. Now completely aware of every word, she continued to explain that although the surgeon thought he had removed all the cancer, after further X-rays, a shadow had appeared on the remaining half of his lung, which seemed to be growing rapidly. Mum went on to explain that Dad couldn't withstand another operation and anyway it was felt the cancer had gone too far. She also explained that Dad didn't know, and he wasn't to find out and we should try to make his remaining weeks as good as possible, and we shouldn't get upset in front of him. She would continue to go to work until Dad couldn't manage then she would have time off.

That was it; that was how I was told my Dad was dying. Mum went to bed and told me to do the same. I didn't receive a hug or a kiss goodnight; she didn't even say she was there if I needed to talk to her, nothing. I went to bed shortly after Mum, but I couldn't sleep. I would begin to drop off and suddenly wake up thinking about my Dad, then drift off only to wake again, this time reliving the incident with Matthew.

The first-week Dad was home, with continued unrest at night, and having to face Dad and pretend as if nothing was wrong was taking its toll on me and I found I would fall asleep whenever I sat down. By the second week Dad's condition hadn't changed, and Mum was still going to work. By the middle of the third week, he started with what seemed to be a cold, but Mum told me that it was more likely to be the start of his decline. Despite this, Mum continued to go to work and left me to look after Dad. I didn't mind, because it gave me time with him and it was the school summer holidays.

I was still only a child, and the stress was becoming unbearable. I felt I was waiting for my Dad to die, which was awful. Every moment I was tormented with fear that something might happen to him. I tried so many times to push the fear of death to the back of my mind, but it wouldn't go away, how could it? Each day I wondered if this would be the last, but I had no-one to talk to about my fears and so they just grew. What would I do and how would I cope if Mum wasn't here at the end? I didn't want Dad to die and I was frightened of seeing him die if I was the only one here. I watched him sleeping in the chair and wondered if I was selfish or just scared. Where would I be if I didn't have my Dad to love and be loved; he was the only one that cared. I was so concerned that I shouldn't get upset in front of Dad, I used to go outside into the garden to get some quite time away from him where I could cry without the worry of him seeing me.

One day I had got upset and ran outside into the shed, closing the door behind me and sobbed. My heart was breaking because I could see no improvement in Dad's health and I was scared of what was going to happen to him. I was suddenly aware that the door was being opened. I dried my eyes quickly, thinking it was Dad coming to find me. As the door opened, I was shocked to see Matthew standing in the doorway, with the garden fork in his hand. I hadn't noticed him in the garden, and so I asked him to excuse me and went to walk past, but my exit was blocked. My heart was thumping in my chest as I told him I had to check on Dad and tried to push past him; Matthew was about sixteen stone, five feet three inches tall. He told me he only wanted to put the fork away and as he went to hang it up he closed the shed door blocking my exit. I told him I needed to get back to the house and went to move past him. He looked at me and smiled, the smile that I had seen before, but did not move so I could leave. He asked me how Dad was, and I told him Dad was ok, but I must get back to him because if he woke up and I wasn't there, he would be worried about me. He replied that Dad would probably still be asleep and not to worry about him. As he came closer to me, I had a sick feeling in the pit of my stomach, dreading what was coming next if I couldn't get out of the shed. I told him I would scream if he didn't let me go; I called him a dirty old man and I would hit him if he did not move. As I moved to strike him he put one hand over my mouth, grabbing my arm with the other hand. I tried to scream out, but it was impossible.

All I could think about was my Dad and that I couldn't get to him if he needed me. I knew if he had known what was happening, he would have protected me from this vile man who only cared about satisfying his own lecherous desires. I realised he had managed to latch the shed door as he pushed me against the workbench. I begged and pleaded with him to let me go, but he just laughed. He told me he loved me, and this time, he would show me just what his love meant. He was suddenly like an octopus; his hands were all over me; it didn't matter how I struggled; I couldn't get free. He kept his hand over my mouth, and with the other hand, he pulled up my tee shirt and undid my bra. He told me while fondling my breasts that he hadn't seen such a large and perfect pair of tits on anyone before. He undid my jeans and pulled them down with my knickers until they reached my knees. I tried to keep my knees closed, but I didn't have the strength. As we fought, one of his fingernails caught the inside of my thigh; as we struggled I managed to knock him off balance and in doing so freed my hands which had been trapped behind me through the sheer force of his weight as he pushed against me. I managed to grab his ear and I pulled as hard as I could which must have hurt as he eased his grip and yelped. I took the advantage and managed to pull free from his hold, yanked my jeans up and opened the door and ran towards the house as fast as I could go. My heart was beating so fast I thought it would come out of my chest, I just needed to get to the safety of the house.

Thank goodness Dad was still asleep and had not missed me, being none the wiser to what had happened. I wished he was well enough for me to have told him what had occurred, but Matthew had told me that Dad was weak, and any shock or upset was likely to kill him. I was so mixed up I didn't know what to do; I dreaded another altercation with Matthew, but if I told Mum, Matthew said she wouldn't believe me, and I knew he was probably right, and I knew I couldn't tell Dad. I had a bath hoping that it would make me feel cleaner, but no matter how much I scrubbed myself, it didn't take away the mental anguish I felt.

These episodes with Matthew started to become a regular occurrence. He would catch me unawares, always when Mum was out and would abuse me at various levels of severity. He told me how much he loved me and this was our secret and I shouldn't tell anyone. Sometimes he would caress my breasts, and sometimes he would pull my jeans down and touch me. I lived on my nerves, never knowing when he may accost me and succumb me to his perverse "affection". There was no one I could confide in, and even if there had been, I don't think I would have done as I was so sure I would not be believed.

It was roughly six and a half weeks since Dad had come home, and his condition hadn't changed. The cold that Mum had said was probably the start of the decline was, in fact, just a cold. Mum made an appointment with Dad's consultant, and I was desperate to go with them, but Mum would not allow it. I even offered to do all the housework, cooking, washing and ironing for a week, but still, the answer was no. The appointment was at four thirty, so I resigned myself to the fact that I would cook tea for when they returned. This seemed like a good idea until I realised I had to go to the freezer, and I didn't want to go to the shed as it held a fear of what might happen again, but I knew Mum would give me a hard time if I hadn't prepared tea. Matthew didn't leave work until half past four, and he was rarely home before five. I looked at the clock; it was quarter to five so I thought I'd have plenty of time as it would only take me a couple of minutes to go to the freezer.

I left the kitchen and quickly walked to the shed. At first, I couldn't find what I was looking, but eventually, at the bottom of the freezer, I found the faggots. I shut the freezer door and turned to leave, but my worst fear had been realised, Matthew was making his way towards the shed. As he came into the shed I shouted at him, 'Not this time, you dirty old man,' and threw the frozen faggots at him. I picked up anything I could reach to throw at him, but he just laughed, smiling at me as someone who knew exactly what they wanted. I realised it was pointless to throw things or try to push past him, he was far too strong and I realised I couldn't get away from him. Matthew closed the shed door behind him and I moved to the furthest end of the shed telling him Mum and Dad would be back any moment; if he went away now, I wouldn't say anything, but if he carried on, I'd tell Mum everything this time.

Matthew was at arm's length from me, and I knew I had to do something to stop him. I reached behind me in a desperate attempt to find something to hit him with while not taking my eyes off him for a second. I grabbed a piece of wood, brought my arm around, and aimed directly at the side of his head. I thought from the thudding noise of the impact, it was all over. Although I was only thirteen years old, I was strong, it didn't matter that I thought I had killed him. However, the reality was a glancing blow that excited him even more.

I realised I had only one action left open to me, which was to kick him in the testicles as hard as I could. I brought my foot up but didn't have the room to achieve the desired impact. Matthew just laughed and told me I didn't want to do that because I loved him. He continued to say that he was about to make me feel so good, and not to be frightened because before he had finished, I would be begging for more. He then touched my face, and I froze. My emotions were all over the place, but fear overcame me. I couldn't shout or scream; I couldn't move or cry; I'd become paralysed with fear, numb from the neck down with only my mind working, racing trying to find a way out of this situation.

Matthew dragged me to the other side of the shed, tied my hands behind my back with his tie and he told me to watch, feel and enjoy what he was going to do. I opened my mouth to scream, but nothing came out, and Matthew instantly gagged me with his handkerchief. With my hands tied and my mouth gagged, I watched in horror as this man slowly and meticulously undid every one of my shirt buttons, then pushed it back over my shoulders and down my arms. He slowly stroked the top of my shoulders, sliding down over my breasts. He looked at them and then into my eyes and told me he would get pleasure from them later.

I prayed for Mum and Dad to return.

He continued by undoing my trousers, pulling them down to my ankles, and removing my pants. I tried desperately to move and kick out; inside I shouted, "Please God help me", but nothing happened. It was awful, I was trapped and couldn't move, and I couldn't even make a noise.

Matthew was standing directly in front of me, my pants and trousers pulled down. He looked at me and told me this was the part I would enjoy. He proceeded to undo his trousers and remove his penis. He told me to watch as he started to masturbate, but I closed my eyes. He shouted at me to open them because if I didn't watch, it would be worse for me. I watched as his penis became harder and more erect and listened to the filth as he explained what would happen next. As he came closer, I felt his penis on my thighs. He asked if I thought it was nice and if I would like to feel it inside me, but first, he wanted to remove my bra, which he did. He played with my right breast, squeezing, sucking, and pinching my nipple until it hurt. With the other hand, he continued to pump his penis and then began to push it between my thighs but not enter my vagina.

He had released his penis and was concentrating on my breasts with both hands. He became rough and began to push his penis harder and quicker between my thighs, simultaneously biting my nipples, which caused so much pain, tears ran from my eyes. Suddenly he stopped; I thought perhaps he had heard Mum, but he had stopped to make me sit on a stool. I sat there, stripped of my dignity, while he began once again to masturbate. My head hung down. He told me that the best was about to come and that I should look up; if I didn't, he would hurt me. I did as I was told, and he removed the gag from my mouth, but it was replaced with his penis. I gagged as it filled my mouth, so awful; it smelt and tasted disgusting. I couldn't move because I was trapped, and he kept pushing it in and out of my mouth. It was hitting the back of my throat and cutting off my breathing.

The rhythm became stronger and faster, and he kept telling me it wouldn't be long and the best was about to come. Suddenly, a surge of semen was forced down my throat, I started to cough as the force pushed it down my nose. I struggled, and Matthew withdrew his penis allowing the remaining semen to hit my face and breasts. I sat there wondering what would happen next and realised I'd wet myself. Matthew was leaning against the shed wall with his eyes closed, then opened his eyes and looked straight at me. He told me it was the best sex he had had in a long time, and the next time would be even better. I wanted to ask if I could go, but the words wouldn't come out.

Matthew untied me and left the shed without saying a word, leaving me sitting on the stool, motionless and in fear of his return. I heard him unlock his back door, but I wasn't sure if this was part of the game he was playing. I couldn't see what was happening, so I could only hope he had gone. I tried to dress myself, but found it almost impossible, as my arms, legs and even my fingers had lost co-ordination. Desperately fighting the fear that he may return at any moment, I managed to pull up my pants and trousers, and re-arrange my blouse. I wanted to scream, but I was too frightened to make any noise, and so my tears fell in silence. A kaleidoscope of emotions racked my mind and body. Fear, disbelief, hurt and total confusion.

Eventually, I had the courage to leave the shed and run to the kitchen, locking the door behind me. I rushed to the bathroom and was violently sick, wanting to rid myself of the filth Matthew had forced upon me. I needed to clean myself of any trace of him, but no matter how much I washed, I couldn't wash away the stain of the abuse. I felt so unclean and desperately needed to tell Mum what was happening to me so she could do something to make it stop.

I was thirteen years old, and naively I had thought Matthew was someone I could trust. Friendships did not come easily; he was the first friend, other than my Dad, I had made since Sam and Jack some eight years before. This man destroyed my trust and took advantage of my vulnerability. He abused me both physically and mentally, leaving scars which, to this day, some twenty-eight years later, still torment me. His pathetic attempts to tell me that he loved me were just the platitudes of a sadistic, dirty man who got his pleasure from abusing young girls.

The year had been a very difficult period for me; my Mum was dismissive of me, my Dad was dying, and the only person I thought I could turn to at the time was Matthew, and he had abused my trust in the most despicable way. I needed his help and support, but perhaps he saw that as a weakness in me that he could take advantage of. He sexually abused me physically, but the mental anguish of fear, revulsion and degradation caused far more long-term damage. I can never forgive him for the pain he inflicted on me, and I can only hope he did not go on to inflict this on others. In the late 1960s these things were not talked about, so I never reported what had happened to me, but today there is support for victims, and no one should ever feel ashamed of coming forward and reporting any form of abuse. Not dealing with it can destroy your life. Although Mattew physically abused me, to an extent I could heal from that. The bruises would fade, I could wash away the spunk and grime, but the mental anguish never diminished and stayed with me every minute of every day, so this was what hurt the most and made me so angry; I felt betrayed again by someone I should have been able to trust at the very time I needed support as Mum was being very distant towards me, and my Dad was very poorly. Matthew abused me, and I hope he rots in hell for his crime; he raped me, a friend who trusted him and should have been safe in his company. You may ask why I didn't report him, but it was hard in those days. I didn't have a relationship with my mother which would allow me to tell her what had happened. I felt sure she would not believe me and would probably call me a liar and I was just out to cause trouble. There weren't support networks readily available, and I had no idea where to go for help. Anyway, I was made to feel dirty and embarrassed by the whole thing and probably would not have sought help even if I had known where to go. The problem was, I trusted Matthew and look what he did to me, so why would I trust another adult? This dilemma still exists for children who are abused by someone they trust. It takes a brave young person to report abuse. Thank goodness there are now people well-versed in dealing with these situations, but still, children are being let down and left to tolerate hideous exploitation. For any young person reading this, and feels they have been abused, I implore them to seek help and support. Speak to someone, you will be believed; times have changed and no-one should feel ashamed or unable to speak about abuse inflicted on them by an adult.

I had no idea what time Mum and Dad arrived home from the hospital, as I was too worried about the reaction I would get from Mum because tea wasn't ready. She had a moan but forgave me when I told her I had been sick and didn't feel well. Dad settled in his usual chair and with the TV on, was ready for a cup of tea. In the kitchen I asked Mum what the specialist had said and that I had something I wanted to tell her, but she said she hadn't time and would talk to me after Dad had gone to bed as she needed to make tea. I returned to the lounge with a cup of tea for Dad, sat with him as he watched the TV. I felt so sorry for him and for me at the thought of losing him I started to fill up with tears. I didn't want him to see me upset as he would have worried, so I went to the bathroom and shed my tears out of sight. The thought of Matthew and what he was doing to me stayed with me all the time. I was so angry with him for the abuse he was inflicting on me, I was angry with my Dad because he was going to die and so angry with Mum for not having time to listen to me. I knew Mum wouldn't talk to me after Dad had gone to bed; she'd go around to see Matthew like she always did. I had to stop her from doing that. I cleaned myself up, dried my eyes and went back into the kitchen and asked her when we could talk. She said she would have a word with Matthew later, and she would talk to me first. This eased my panic, but I was still worried how I would tell her what had happened, and whether she would believe me, or like Matthew had said, she would think I was lying.

That evening was probably the longest evening I'd ever known. The minutes and hours dragged as though time was standing still. At last, Mum had put Dad to bed, and she came from the kitchen with a cup of tea. She settled herself on the settee and told me what the specialist had said. Although I desperately wanted to hear about Dad, I also knew I must tell Mum what had happened before I lost my nerve. I interrupted her, saying I had something important to tell her, but she rebuked me, asking if I wanted to know about Dad. When I said I did, she told me to listen and not be so rude by interrupting her. I suddenly felt guilty for not wanting to listen; after all, she was going to tell me about Dad, but as much as I wanted to know, I had to tell her about Matthew as quickly as possible. I took a deep breath and I tried to calm down and listen to her. Mum explained that the specialist had taken a number of x-rays, and nothing had changed. There still appeared to be an enlarged area, but it hadn't grown anymore. Mum continued to say Dad wasn't going to die and that the reason he hadn't seemed any better was because he suffered with his chest, so the lungs would take longer to recover from the operation. In addition, Dad was suffering from a chest infection, but he should recover with antibiotics.

I was so relieved at this news; it was suddenly the end of a nightmare that had tormented me day and night. I had been dreading each day may be the last, and I always had a knot in my stomach never sure what was going to happen. It had been so hard watching Dad suffering with his health and not seeming to get any better. I loved and respected him so very much, and pretending for his sake that nothing was wrong had been hard. I desperately wanted to hug him and tell him that I loved him and I'd always be there for him. To say how sad I was for all the time we had apart when I was little, and I was sorry for any upset I may have caused him.

I should have been elated, but all I felt was numb, devoid of all emotion. The utter relief of knowing Dad was not going to die imminently was like a weight being lifted, but it left me in a state of confusion between being grown up and being a child. For so long I had adulthood thrust upon me, taking responsibility for Dad's care, when I should have been with my friends enjoying my childhood. Dad was going to be okay; he was going on a course of antibiotics and then he would be fine. How had Mum got this so wrong? Why, when all Dad had was a chest infection, had she been telling me of his probable death. I felt yet again she had been playing me to her own advantage, giving her the time she craved to spend with Matthew.

Mum's voice brought me back with a start as I heard her say, "You wanted to tell me something." To be honest, I wasn't sure if I wanted to tell her about the incident with Matthew, but before I could think, I had told her it didn't matter, it wasn't important. With this, Mum got up from the settee and said, "In that case, I'm just going to pop around to Matthew and tell him the news. I'll be back just now." I suppose hearing Matthew's name jolted me into action. I called Mum back and immediately started to cry. She didn't come and sit beside me on the settee but took the chair opposite. I told her about every episode of Matthews's abuse towards me and where they had taken place. She sat emotionless and listened to every sobbing word I mumbled. For once, she was taking notice of me and appeared to be listening to every word, although I really wanted her to hug me and give me some reassurance. Speaking about this was one of the hardest things I had ever had to do, and the loneliness I felt almost overwhelmed me.

I finally finished telling her everything that had happened to me. My eyes were sore, my face wet from tears and my nose and top lip were covered with mucus. Mum just continued to sit there, not saying a word, with her eyes focused directly on me. I expected her to show some reaction to what I had said; repulsion, anger, pain, but nothing; she just stared at me. I remained seated, with Mum staring at me. Eventually, I got up to get a tissue, and as I walked across the lounge, she told me in a calm voice that she didn't believe a word that I had said. That I was a liar, and she didn't want to hear another word, and furthermore, if I told Dad, she would ensure I was sent away. She then got up and left to go and see Matthew.

The subject of Matthew's abuse towards me never came up again, but strangely, there was never a recurrence after that night. I will never know if Mum said anything to him and whether she did in fact believe me. At the time it appeared to me, as far as Mum was concerned, she had heard the story and closed the book and there was nothing else to say. If only it could have been that simple for me, but I was tormented by what had happened to me, and I had to learn to live with it.

I was physically abused, mentally drained, and I had a mother who didn't believe or care what had happened to me. This wasn't an ideal situation for a child to live in, but thank goodness my Dad wasn't going to die. Without him and the knowledge that he loved me, and sanctuary of my bedroom where I could find some peace and respite, I couldn't have carried on. As days passed and, other than at mealtimes, I only talked to Dad, as I had nothing to say to Mum and she ignored me most of the time, unless it was to ask me to do some household chores. I became more isolated, staying in my room or going to the woods opposite the house, where I would sit for hours on one of the oak trees watching others living their carefree, happy lives. I saw children playing together; people walking their dogs, in easy conversation with one another, relaxed and happily enjoying the countryside. I was desperate for affection and to be told everything was alright; what had happened with Matthew wasn't my fault, I was the child, and he was the adult, a grown man who should never have taken advantage of a child in that way. I knew I should tell my Dad what had happened but talking about the abuse to a man would be difficult, even though it was my Dad. I still felt dirty and ashamed of the things Matthew had done to me, and I wasn't sure I would ever have been able to tell him what had taken place over the past few months. One day, I plucked up the courage, sat beside Dad and told him I wanted to talk to him. But my resolve evaporated as soon as he put down his newspaper and looked at me with concern on his face, "What's up love?" I instantly knew I couldn't tell him all the vile things Matthew had done; what if he didn't believe me and, like Mum, thought I was lying. A voice inside told me not to tell him; it will make things worse, so I made some feeble excuse that I needed to check something before speaking to him. I went to my bedroom, knowing I had done the right thing as I couldn't risk further rejection, but in my heart, believing my Dad would never have rejected me as my Mum had, but too frightened to risk it.

Reality hit me and I knew, I had to protect myself from the effects of loneliness, isolation, rejection, and abuse. Although I was only thirteen and still a child, I understood I had to put some sort of defence around myself, and the only way I knew how to do that, was to put a mental wall between me and my emotions. Like the shield put around a young sapling to protect it from predators, my "wall" would protect me from further harm. Loneliness would no longer be my enemy if I accepted the protection of the wall. At that age I did not understand the damage this action would do to me in later life; my "wall" would govern future friendships and stop me from getting close to anyone, remaining distant and unemotional. But at the time I was determined no one would hurt me again, and I thought this would be achieved by building my wall which would prevent anyone getting too close to me, not understanding the long-term consequences. I felt my childhood had finally ended with the destruction of innocence leaving me with no choice other than to protect myself the only way I knew how.

The weeks eventually turned into months, and, to be honest, time didn't have any meaning anymore. My fourteenth birthday had been and gone. Except for a card, some money from my Dad and three pairs of pants from Mum which weren't even wrapped, it was like any other day. I loved that Dad had given me a card, and he said, "I know it's not much, and I'm sorry I couldn't get out to get you a present, but you can buy yourself something nice". I hugged him for being so kind and promised I would buy something special.

As July came, it meant it was time for our summer holiday at the farm. I always looked forward to these weeks, but this time, I couldn't wait. It wasn't just because I felt Sussex was my home; I also had a certain amount of freedom when we were there, so didn't feel so affected by Mum's uncaring attitude. It was obvious to me by her actions that she didn't love me and either didn't or didn't want to see how I was suffering by what was now becoming controlling behaviour. She had become obsessed with me, wanting to rule my every thought and movement. I'm sure she saw me as a puppet on a string, answering to her beck and call. When she told me about Philip, my biological Dad, she had said all she ever wanted was a child to love, but now in all honesty I doubt that sentiment. To be honest I think she wanted someone to control and who better than me? Although my "brick wall" had started to work and was protecting me, I found that Mum prayed on my conscience. I began to question my feelings toward her. After all she was my Mum, and surely it was only natural to feel some affection for your mother. I couldn't understand why there was no bond between us, but I had no memories of affection from her to build on and so no basis to develop a relationship with her. I knew in my heart I had nothing to feel guilty for and could only think it was something to do with the fact she had dismissed my accusations about Matthew out of hand, clearly showing she believed Matthew over me. Whatever the reason, I couldn't stop the feeling that she had let me down.

The third week in July came, and we arrived at the farm after a six-hour hot and sticky journey, but after a good night's sleep and a hearty breakfast the next morning, I was ready to start exploring. My uncle owned five fields, three being on the same side as the farmhouse and two directly opposite. A twisty lane separated these fields from the house, with the entrance on the bend giving just enough room to stand off the road. I crossed over and climbed the five-bar gate and jumped down; standing for a moment I looked at the open space, my eyes resting on the far corner of the field. Several minutes later after walking around the perimeter of the field to avoid ruining the crops, I reached the corner and instantly recognised the noise of water trickling over pebbles and stones. I walked to a clearing where my uncle came to pick watercress, which grew in abundance. The stream was no more than a foot deep, and as I had borrowed Norma's wellingtons, so I slid down the bank into the water. Although it was a hot summer day, the water felt cold and tingled my feet through my wellingtons, bringing a sense of calmness and peace. I started to walk in the direction the water was running and soon became engrossed with its lack of urgency and carefree attitude. I continued walking slowly until I reached the small island that sat directly in the middle path of the stream.

Over many years, with the continuous back flow, the water had created a channel around the island where the water was too deep to walk through.

I stood for a while, watching the water hit the island and turn white as it forced itself against the never-ending current. I moved and sat on the embankment, free from thoughts, watching the water as it made its way downstream. Without wellingtons or socks, I walked in the shallows, the water flowing over my ankles, toes and across my feet. Whatever obstacle was placed in its way, the stream only suffered temporary hindrance, the water finding its way around. It felt as though I was watching a free spirit finding freedom. I wondered and mentally asked myself, "Is that what I wanted to become, a free spirit?" Yes, I think perhaps it was. I looked closer at the water for any hidden traps that I may not have noticed, but there weren't any. This water was as free as a bird that flies in the sky; it had no ruler other than nature, and at times it had to change direction, but it was happy doing what water does just going quietly on its way. Why couldn't life be that simple? Why couldn't I be like that stream? To be a free spirit, just following the flow; for once not being hurt, to be loved, to have genuine friends and to be happy. For a moment, I wondered what was the purpose of this stream; I asked the same question about myself, but I couldn't answer either.

For the two weeks of the holiday, I became preoccupied with sitting by the stream, which became my hideaway. It was total peace, and a place that I felt a certain bond with, somewhere I could sit and work out just how I felt, and above all try to learn something about myself, my family and my life. I've always believed in God, but over the years I had started to reject what he stood for and questioned his motives for allowing people to suffer, and that included me. I suppose I felt he had let me down and I had to find some other help by any means I could. If that meant hours in my bedroom at home, or here by the stream, thinking and trying to understand what was happening to me, then perhaps that's how it had to be.

Before I realised it, being too occupied with my safe place of retreat, my holiday was almost over. I really didn't want to return home, although I had missed my bedroom as it was my only other safe place. The rest of the house brought nothing but sadness and torment, and I dreaded returning. The day before we were due to leave the farm, I asked Norma if it was alright with her, if could I stay the remainder of the school holidays. I knew it wasn't any good asking auntie because she wasn't bothered with me, but I got on with Norma, and I knew she understood a little about how I felt. She managed to persuade Mum that she would take care of me, and Mum grudgingly agreed to let me remain for another four weeks. When I realised I could stay, I didn't thank Norma until much later but ran immediately to the stream like a child running to join their playmate and shouted, "It's alright, I'm back, and I can stay." Momentarily, when I reached the stream, I felt a strange feeling I couldn't explain, but now I realise I had experienced the joy of happiness for the first time.

Norma tried her utmost to encourage me to go shopping and on day trips with her, but I wasn't interested. All I wanted was to spend time at the stream, until eventually I didn't even bother returning to the farm much before dusk.

At fourteen, I'd become a bit of a recluse; I didn't know anything else, so I suppose it was inevitable. I'd missed my childhood, which was supposed to be the most carefree years of your life, and I should have been going through the stages of adolescence, but I seemed to be missing that stage as well. Physically, I'd started my periods when I was nine years old, and according to the rules of nature, I was now a woman. Mum had never talked to me about periods or growing up, and she had certainly never spoken to me about sex. I'd learnt nothing about life; I didn't know what it was like to have a loving relationship with my parents or how to make friends, fallout and make up again. I didn't know how to read and write, cook and shop, or the value of money. I had learnt nothing other than what hurt felt like. I'd become a woman that lived in a child's body, but I had no idea how to behave or to have self-respect as I did not understand who I was. I knew I was no longer a child, but with little or no experience in life, I couldn't believe I was grown up. I couldn't say I'd lost myself because I'd never found my identity in the first place. I felt I was made up of bits joined together; part of me was a woman, and part of me still a child.

Day after day at the stream, I continued to question, and try to understand, even learn just who I was. I knew I had only three weeks left in which to find my inner self before I had to return home, but I also knew if I didn't achieve it by then, I never would. Questions followed by more questions, answers that contradicted previous answers, tears that dried and then were replaced with others, and mental anguish that wouldn't stop. It had become a vicious circle, and somewhere in there, was me, not that crazy mixed-up person on the exterior, but the real me.

One issue I had to deal with was the fact that I was gay. Although at a very early age I knew there was something different with me, and that I was attracted to women, I didn't understand what this meant, and it certainly was not talked about. I had endured many emotional disturbing events in my life, and felt I had very little control over my own life. Perhaps I thought I was gay because it was a choice I could make for myself, but of course I now realise your sexuality is not a choice, it is something you are born with. My time at the stream allowed to question the issue of sexuality, but I was too young to comprehend the significance of my feelings, and it just left me feeling more confused.

I recall one afternoon becoming conscious of my surroundings and looked around but couldn't see anything out of the ordinary. I checked my watch, it was 4:30 pm but it wasn't time to go back to the farm. I turned back towards the stream and drifted into thought again. I was thinking about being gay. I was about twelve years old when I first had a crush on someone, and like many children, it was a crush on a teacher, but the difference was my attraction was for someone of the same sex. Mum had explained, in a way, about the birds and the bees and what I should and shouldn't do, but she never spoke about feelings, and how they may affect you. As I didn't know anything about gay people, I didn't know what to expect or to understand how I was feeling. It wasn't a subject openly talked about in those days, other than the odd comment that they were dirty, abnormal people, it was never discussed.

Now, two years on, being fourteen and a half my feelings towards other women became stronger, I realised my emotions weren't just towards my teacher, but towards women in general. I was confused, I didn't know what I wanted to do. On one hand, I felt I wanted to be with a woman, but on the other hand I knew it was wrong. I also felt I was the only one that had these types of feelings. I thought people would argue that the reason I thought I was gay, was due to the bad experience with Matthew. I have asked that question myself, but these emotions started two years before the episodes with Matthew, and so I knew it had nothing to do with it.

Still sitting by the stream, with another day nearly ending, I began to wonder if I would ever find an answer to my questions. What would I do if I couldn't? But my head was aching from too many questions and not enough answers. Perhaps I was trying to find something that wasn't there. Maybe I was born to be a loser, a person without an identity, that other people felt they could step on and abuse whenever they wanted to, and ridicule because I was gay. It wasn't the answer I wanted, but it was the only one that made any sense. Disappointed at my conclusion, I eased myself from the embankment back into the water and began walking, not realising I was going in the wrong direction from the farm.

It wasn't long before I realised my mistake, so I decided to walk across the field instead of going back along the stream. Suddenly, a voice from behind caught my attention. I turned and noticed Andrew Bogel running up toward me. His father owned the neighbouring farm. At sixteen, Andrew was about two years older than me. We had never been friends in all the time we had known each other, but we had always spoken. He guessed I was down here on my holidays, and for some reason, I offered the information I was here for a further three weeks. He asked the usual questions; where I had been and what I had been doing. I told him the truth, telling him I sat by the stream most of the day. We crossed the field and entered his Dad's farmyard. Andrew insisted on walking up the lane to aunties with me because it was now quite dark. I thanked him and never gave him another thought.

The minute I walked in, Norma read the riot act about being late, saying it wasn't fair on her worrying where I was, and in the future, I was to come back at a more reasonable time. I suppose I could understand her concerns and promised that I wouldn't do it again. I really wanted someone to talk to about what was on my mind. I knew Norma would have listened, she was the fairest person I knew, but I felt she probably wouldn't have understood, so I said nothing.

A couple of weeks passed, and I spent most of my time sitting at the streams edge, but now my thoughts were being interrupted by visits from Andrew. He was a friendly lad, and he obviously enjoyed some company, but I didn't want the intrusion into my space and couldn't be honest and tell him, so I begrudgingly accepted these interruptions.

The time on my own became less and less, until one day Andrew didn't turn up. For a few hours, I was grateful to be able to drift in and out of my own thoughts without being bothered by trivial chatter, but around dinnertime, I realised I had actually missed his company and light-heartedness. I didn't consider him a friend, but someone that was just there, who talked none stop. The following day Andrew reappeared, although he never explained why he had not come the day before, and I didn't ask. He joined me by the stream each day, not wanting to rush off doing what boys of that age do but was quite content sitting by the stream with me, watching and listening. He wasn't like any other boy I had ever met.

It was some days later that the confused, angry, and hurt child I was, tried to become a woman. In doing so, I would suffer anguish that haunted me for the rest of my life. You see, it had started to become dusk and as usual Andrew and I walked towards his Dad's farm. We would typically cross the field into the yard, but this day as we passed the hay barn, Andrew asked if I wanted to see the new chicken shed that his Dad had just finished building. We made our way towards it as Andrew explained that it would eventually hold about twenty chickens, but his Dad didn't intend to buy any until later in the season. After looking at the outside, we decided to go inside. I suppose to us, it was more like a den than a chicken shed. Once inside, we closed the door and sat down on the clean straw. Andrew continued talking about something stupid, and before long I realised I had started to laugh. For most people, this emotion is something they take for granted and comes quite naturally, but for me, it didn't, and so finding myself laughing was an unusual experience and one that I liked, although the feeling of sadness wasn't that far away.

I can't really recall just how it happened, but one thing led to another, and Andrew and I ended up making love on the chicken shed floor. Perhaps

I shouldn't call it making love because we were both too young and inexperienced. I suppose teenage sex, or physical exploration probably describes it better.

Having sex wasn't something that had crossed my mind, let alone wanted to try. Looking back, I was very confused, but one thing I was sure about, was that I wanted someone to love me. I don't mean sexually, but to feel wanted and loved. I suppose it was only inevitable when Andrew held me in his arms, I became confused and had no idea what I was doing. To this day, I can't explain the conflicting emotions that I felt at the time. I suppose if it could have stayed at a cuddle, then it would have been better, and really, that's all I wanted. For once in my life, it felt good to receive so much warmth and attention and to finally feel that someone really cared. Unfortunately, from this, my virginity was lost, and so was the warmth and love that I had felt. It had been replaced with an overwhelming surge of anger. The anger was not with Andrew but with me. Why had I done something I didn't want to, and why had I let it go beyond a kiss and a cuddle?

Following our sexual encounter, my emotions and thoughts were confused. I was not blaming Andrew, but I questioned myself for allowing this to happen. The physical act, which I did not truly understand, felt like a mix of revenge on my Mum and Matthew, wanting to experience a closeness to someone without being intimidated by them and the excitement of my first willing sexual encounter.

Of course, the thought of being gay entered my mind. I still didn't know or understand how I felt, but wondered if the experience with Andrew may help. Years of emotional frustration had taken their toll.

I questioned why at fourteen and a half, I was having sex I didn't want or particularly like. I suppose I misunderstood the need for love and affection with something physical, and all it managed to do was make me even more confused

I suppose you could think Andrew wasn't any different from Matthew. Both, in their own way, had abused or taken advantage of a child. However, I never questioned Andrews' motives as being purely selfish. Yes, he was older than me and should have known better, but he did not force himself onto me in the way that Matthew did; circumstances just got out of control.

I never felt let me down or abused by Andrew. Only my mother and so called friends could hurt me, and as Andrew wasn't a friend, he couldn't hurt me. The question of blame was irrelevant and probably equally shared, but the time spent in his arms before intercourse, made me realise just what it felt to be held, warm and close. It gave me the knowledge that something lovely really did exist.

CHAPTER FOUR

Finally, the holiday was over for another year, and I should have been grateful to have been allowed six weeks and not the usual two. I had become accustomed to having more freedom, and I knew this would only make my return home more difficult.

Although some things were still unclear, I had managed to form a conclusion about my sexuality. The experience with Andrew undoubtedly helped me to accept this; I had loved the warmth and closeness, but I had not enjoyed the intercourse. I wasn't happy with the realisation of being gay, but I understood it was something I couldn't help. This was, at last, one step towards sorting my life out. For once, I knew something for definite, but how I was going to deal with it was another matter.

During the next few months, I tried to come to terms with the dilemma of how I was going to tell my Mum I was gay, at the same time trying to ignore the changes in my body that I was noticing almost daily.

By the middle of November, it became obvious I was filling my clothes and, in some cases, out-growing them. Mum was clearly not happy with the prospect of having to buy new clothes and told me I should go on a diet. I should have told her then that I was pregnant, but I did not want to face it until I had to.

As it happened, I didn't have to bring the subject up, as Mum guessed. She asked all the relevant questions, why, who, where and when, but not once did she ask how I felt. I understood she would be angry, but I had hoped she would eventually calm down and give me some moral support.

She had worked out that it must have been while I was at auntie's and asked me if that was right. I knew if I told her the truth, I would never be allowed back at the farm, and as the farm meant freedom which I could not risk losing, I lied and told her it had happened in the first week back at school. As we had never spoken about intimate things, Mum seemed reluctant to discuss my pregnancy in any detail and seemed to accept my explanation. I knew lying to her was wrong, but what choice had I got?

I asked her what would happen and hoped she would explain what I could expect during the next few months and at the birth. Perhaps to tell me what I should and should not do and how to look after myself and the baby. But I received no such guidance; instead she said she would have to think seriously about this situation so she could decide what to do. Of course, at the time I did not fully appreciate the issues surrounding me being pregnant; after all I was only a child myself. But, as usual, I felt let down and neglected by Mum at the very time I needed her support and guidance.

She made me wait approximately a month before giving me her decision, by which time I was nearly five months into my pregnancy. She sat me down and proceeded to tell me that she didn't think it was fair of me to expect her and Dad, especially Dad at his age, to help look after a baby when really, I was no more than a child myself. She pointed out that by the time the baby was born, I would be fifteen, already have left school, and should be looking for a job. She reminded me that Dad wasn't working, and I would need to be responsible for my own keep.

I asked her what she meant, as I didn't understand. On one hand, she was saying, "I was no more than a baby myself," but on the other hand saying that I, "should be looking for a job," and "be responsible for my own keep." It was an innocent question, but I wasn't prepared for the answer that followed. Mum remained seated, just looking at me, her face still, cold and emotionless. Her voice was calm but with a sense of authority that was far- reaching.

She told me that the minute the baby was born, she would have it put up for adoption. The social services would have to be informed because of my age, and they would be making the necessary arrangements for the adoption to take place. I had to see the doctor for a check-up, and so she didn't lose any time from work, this appointment and any future ones would be made out of work hours so she could come with me.

For the next four months, I lived in a state of shock and bewilderment. I wasn't sure what I felt towards Mum; I certainly felt no love, but neither did I have any anger or hatred towards her. I suppose my brick wall had finally worked, no feelings, no hurt, no pain. Dad, as much as I loved him never said a word to me about my pregnancy, but I understood why. Because of his health, Dad relied on Mum a great deal, and over the years, like me, he became an unopinionated, isolated possession under my mother's control. Gradually, Mum manipulated our movements, like pawns in a game of chess she ruled over us, imprisoning us in a world of ownership.

During those four months, I desperately wanted to ask Mum to allow me to keep my baby, but her decision was final, and how I felt didn't come into it. The arrangements had been made by Social Services; when the time came, I was to go to Coventry Hospital. I never understood why it had to be Coventry Hospital, perhaps so I was out of the area for the adoption.

On the thirtieth of April I was taken into Hospital suffering from stomach pains, which turned out to be labour pains. Mum didn't come with me, using Dad as an excuse saying he was not well enough to leave on his own. Mum told me the Social Worker would be with me all the time. She wasn't a very nice woman and hardly spoke to me during the journey to the hospital. The kindest person was one of the nursing sisters when I went into the delivery room. She could see how frightened I was, and she told me what to expect and listen to her and I would be fine.

As kind as the Nurse was, and as much as she tried to help me, I wanted my Mum. Despite everything Mum had ever done to me, and even when she was going to give my baby away, I still wanted her with me. The pain was becoming unbearable, I reached out, half expecting her to hold my hand, but of course I ended up with a nurse's hand instead. All I could hear was someone saying push, and again, and again, now do your breathing, pant, keep panting until the next pain.

I so desperately wanted my Mum with me. More pain, and this time it was worse. Why wasn't Mum with me? She was my Mum, and despite how I felt about her, this was the one time I really needed her. Another wave of pain tore into me. I heard someone say, "take this, it will ease the pain a little." I breathed in the gas, and at the same time a nurse wiped the sweat from my brow. The Sister told me with the next pain, the baby will come if I push hard enough. The pain started, and it became stronger and stronger; I pushed harder and harder, panting between each contraction. I had never known pain like this, but the Sister said, "on the next contraction, push and baby will come."

The final push worked, and my baby was born. A nurse carried it off to the other side of the room. I couldn't see what she was doing, as her body was in front of me. I heard a cry and asked if the baby was alright and was it a boy or a girl. The Nurse told me I had a boy and he was perfectly normal. I wanted to see my baby and asked if I could hold him, but the staff ignored me and left the delivery room with him. I begged to see him but was flatly refused any contact.

My baby was born on 2nd May 1970. All I ever knew was the sex and that he was healthy. The last thing I heard as the door closed was his cry. I cannot begin to explain the emotions I felt, during pregnancy, at the time of the birth, and now, so many years later.

As many women will know, words cannot be found to describe the heartache, pain and mental torment suffered at the loss of a baby. No matter your age, during the nine months of pregnancy your body is preparing you for what should be the most wonderful experience of your life. From morning sickness to heartburn, restless nights to being so tired you can hardly function, from cravings, to being revolted by the smell of some foods. At the end of it, you should have a bundle of joy that fills your heart with warmth and love. But when your baby is taken away, and you are not even allowed to see him, the pain of that loss is both physical and mental and will impact the rest of your life.

Whether the mother has made the decision, or as in my case by someone else, the incredible sense of loss, overwhelming guilt and anger can only be compared to a bereavement. The loss of someone through death is final, and although never forgotten, with the falling of leaves each Autumn, and new life each Spring, you perhaps learn to live with the loss in the knowledge that your loved one is at rest. But with adoption, you can never put that grief to rest. You have no idea where your baby is. Whether he is happy, safe and well with a loving family or has ended up in a loveless home. Someone else is watching him grow up, take his first steps, first day at school and grow into a young man and have a family of his own.

I was shocked at how my instincts to protect my child affected me. I felt empty and like part of me had left with my baby.

I returned home from the hospital a week later, and the following months I merely existed. I felt as though I was walking through a thick fog, not knowing or caring what I was doing. Mum had managed to get me a job where she worked, but I couldn't even remember going to work. All I could think about was my baby and how part of me was forever lost.

As time passed, the fog started to lift, and I began to see things clearer. I started to put all my energies into work. The job was piecework, so I could focus on what I was doing, putting everything else to the back of my mind. I started earning good money and tried to save as much as possible. My goal was to get enough money behind me so that at eighteen, I could leave home and my mother, who I now hated with a passion as I blamed her for my loss. I had so much anger and hatred toward her, and could not understand how she let me go through the pregnancy and birth on my own without any love or support. It now felt as though all she wanted from me was money, which I handed over at the end of each week. She controlled me like she did everyone around her. If I wanted to do anything on my own, she made me feel guilty and told me she could not trust me. She would never forgive me for getting pregnant and was determined to prevent anything happening to me again by controlling my every movement.

The following months I worked at the factory and was earning sixty-five pounds per week after stoppages. This was very good money for someone of my age, but the job was piecework, and I adapted to it very well. Mum insisted that I give her fifteen pounds per week, but soon increased it to twenty-five pounds, which left me with about forty pounds. The trouble was, I had foolishly started to smoke, and after buying my cigarettes and other personal items, I was only left with thirty pounds. But, I opened a bank account and saved as much as possible hoping that I would have enough money to rent somewhere when I was eighteen.

The summer was upon us, and the factory shut down for the last week in July and the first week in August. Our bags were packed, and the holiday destination was the farm. As soon as we arrived, I spent my time by the stream as in previous years, but it didn't seem quite the same. Yes, it still meandered gently on its way, but it didn't have its peaceful and calming effect on me, which was hardly surprising considering what had happened in the past twelve months. I learnt that Andrew Bogel had a girlfriend who he now lived with, so he was not at the farm, which was a relief as I did not relish the thought of seeing him.

It was a strange holiday. The farm, which had always been a sanctuary for me, giving me freedom and tranquillity, seemed to have lost its magic. The trees, fields and animals were still there; the watercress still grew in abundance along the stream bed, but I felt restless. I sat by the stream during the day, trying to recapture the composure I had felt the previous year, but to no avail. While I marvelled at the nature all around me, it no longer gave me the space to think; my mind would not settle, constantly moving from one thought to the next, never giving me time to contemplate.

Auntie was now the manageress of the social club. In the evening she would go to work, and sometimes I would go with her. I remember the main room had big leather chairs and a bar at the far end. There were two other rooms, one had three snooker tables and the other had a dance floor and disco, which was rarely used. The rooms always looked dark and dingy, but despite this, the club always did well.

One night, auntie asked if I would go to work with her, as she needed some help because her back was playing up. I agreed, but I am not sure whether it was to genuinely help auntie or to get away from Mum, I suspect the latter.

When I wasn't collecting glasses and washing up, I sat in the corner with a packet of Crawford cheese biscuits, and although too young to drink, I had managed to sneak half a lager and lime. Although I didn't know the locals, they were all very friendly when they knew Cissi was my auntie, but most of the time I sat quietly on my own watching and listening to conversations which were nothing to do with me. Later on in the evening the club became quite busy, and I moved seats to a table on my own in a quieter area of the room. Really this was to give me more space as I was beginning to feel closed in by the number of people. A short time after this, a young chap came into the club, I suppose he was about seventeen. He bought himself a drink and then, to my surprise, came and sat down next to me, and introduced himself as Trevor. As my social skills were not good, I found it very difficult to make polite conversation, but Trevor chatted away and I found myself relaxing. He obviously knew Cissi was my auntie and told me he lived at Burgess Hill and his father owned the garage, which was opposite my Gran's bungalow. Although he had never known my Grandad, he knew my Gran and had kind words to say about her. He bought us both a drink and we chatted on until it was time to close, and I went to help Auntie wash the glasses and tidy up.

I went to the club with Auntie the following night, and Trevor was there again. He offered to buy me a drink and keep me company. Before long, he started telling me about the local people he knew, and to my surprise, I began to join in. We talked about my auntie and Uncle, and Norma and Barbara. We both remembered Victoria Sands; she lived next door to Gran, and half the time she was so drunk she didn't know whether she was on foot or horseback.

Although Trevor was two years older than me, we had both attended Cross in Hand School. We agreed the school was alright other than dinner time. Although purpose-built, it had no facilities for cooking and dining, so other arrangements were made. At noon each day, the children were asked to form two rows in the playground, boys on the right and girls on the left. From the playground, we marched out of the school yard for about three hundred yards. Arriving at our destination, which I can only describe as a corrugated green tin shack, and probably had a condemned sticker on it somewhere, we were packed into a room like sardines. We both remembered the food was as grim as the "canteen", but recalled that, along with our classmates, we ate everything put in front of us. For many children this was the only hot meal of the day, showing that school dinners were as important back then as they are today.

Trevor and I continued to chatter, laughing about the drunken antics of Victoria Sands, the primitive school dining shack, and memories we both had of our childhoods. I realised I was enjoying spending time with Trevor, finding conversation easy, something I had never experienced. Before we realised, Auntie was calling time, and it was time to go home. I only had one day of my holiday left, and as Trevor already had plans for the following evening, he asked if we could exchange addresses and write to each other.

To my surprise, a week after returning home, I received a letter from Trevor. He said how much he had enjoyed our time together, talking about school, places, and people we both knew. He hoped I was well, and would I write to him, which of course, I did.

We kept in touch, writing each month, but this soon progressed to a letter every week. I had only seen Trevor at the club when I was with Auntie, so Mum did not know about our growing friendship. I wasn't sure about my feelings for Trevor, but I knew that I liked him; he reminded me of myself, and of the only place I really thought of as home, which was the farm. But in truth, I am not sure if I wrote to him because I really wanted to, or because it made me feel as though I had something Mum knew nothing about.

As the months passed, I realised that all my priorities had changed. For years I wanted and searched for my mother's love, which had never materialised. Now, all the love I once felt toward her had turned to hate. I desperately wanted my baby son, and all I knew was it was down to Mum that he had been taken away from me. She had never talked to me about the pregnancy, the birth or what would happen to the baby. It was taken out of my hands, almost as though it was nothing to do with me. I was shown no compassion by anyone during this period; I realise now that I was grieving a loss, that probably only a mother can truly understand. It was even harder to deal with at my young age, as I had no one to support or listen to me. I didn't want my mother's love anymore; I was far too bitter and angry to accept it, even if it had been offered.

I continued to work hard and saved as much money as I could. I looked forward to receiving letters from Trevor each week, but my son was never far from my mind, and I prayed that one day when he was old enough, he would find me. By acknowledging my mother for who she was, meant the torment of not having her love lessoned.

In November, Trevor wrote and asked if I was going down to my aunties for the Christmas holiday. I wrote back, explaining normally I wouldn't be down again until next summer, but I would ask Mum if I could come down for Christmas this year. The more I thought about it, the more I wanted to go. I asked Mum if she had considered going, but her answer was no, as expected.

Christmas is a time of goodwill; for giving and receiving gifts. All I could think was that I should be buying presents for my son on his first Christmas and putting them under the tree ready for Christmas Day. This would have been our first Christmas together, and without him, I didn't want to spend it at home with my mother.

I decided to telephone Norma from the phone box as we were not on the phone at home. I asked her if I could come down for Christmas week; she told me I could if Mum agreed. I rushed home to ask Mum, but of course, she refused. She gave me a lecture about how Christmas was a time for families to be together, and she thought this year she would invite Matthew for both Christmas and Boxing Day, so she really needed my help.

The thought of spending Christmas with not only Mum, but Matthew as well, was too much. I decided I would go down to the farm anyway and planned to book my bus ticket in advance. The factory closed down two days before Christmas Day and as I had already booked my ticket at the bus station, I was ready to go. I'd packed my bags and told Mum I didn't care what she said, and I was going to aunties'. Mum told me that the minute I walked out of the door, she would inform the police and they would bring me straight back. We argued back and forth until I said I hated her for all she had ever done to me. I told her she didn't love me, because if she did, she wouldn't have treated me the way she had and that she would have believed me about Matthew. And now you expect me sit in the same room with him at Christmas.

I told her, I had as much respect for her as she had for me; that I had loved her once, but she had destroyed my love in so many ways, but the thing I hated her for the most, was giving my baby away. This Christmas, I should be spending here with my son, but no thanks to her, that would not happen. I asked her, "How do you think I'm feeling, or don't you care?" I went on to tell her no matter what she said or did, I was going to Aunties; I said, "If you want to inform the police then do so, at least that way I may go into care and probably be loved and understood better." At this point, Mum told me to go to my room and not to come down until I could talk to her with respect. By now, I had started to say whatever came into my mind, I didn't care if it hurt her or what the consequences might be; I just had to get all this pent-up emotion off my chest.

I went to my room, exhausted and tearful, but a few minutes later, Mum called me down. I don't know what had happened, perhaps some of what I said pricked her conscience, but she agreed to me going to Aunties for Christmas, although she didn't say, "Sorry" or "Try to enjoy yourself." I phoned Auntie to tell her I was coming, assuring her that Mum had agreed to my visit. Mum took me to the bus station, wishing me a Happy Christmas and saying she would ring Auntie later that evening to ensure I had arrived safely. She didn't wait to see the coach leave, so I watched as she returned to the car and drove off, not looking back once. Even though I wanted to go to the Farm, I couldn't help but feel the sting of tears as I watched Mum drive away, and wished with all my heart she had hugged me, told me that she loved me, and to have a good Christmas.

Throughout the holiday, although I spent time with Trevor, which was good, and he made me laugh, I couldn't help but think about all the awful things I'd said to Mum before leaving. I knew in my heart some of what I said was true, but whatever she had done to me, she was still my mother. I started to feel sorry for her and guilty for some of the things I had said. I began to question whether she was to blame or was it me. I was feeling very confused and was determined that when I got home, I would speak to Mum, and clear the air.

However, when I returned home, I paid for my outburst. Dad asked if I was all right and said he had missed me but hoped I had had a good time, but Mum, on the other hand completely ignored me for the first two weeks. She gave me the silent treatment and "sent me to Coventry," not speaking to me other than when necessary. I began to wonder whether it was all my fault, and before long, not understanding the consequences of what I was about to do, I said, "Sorry", which Mum accepted without comment or acknowledgement of any blame.

During the next six months, the friction between us eased and, although Mum was still very possessive towards me, she had mellowed, showing me some affection. I can't say she was understanding or hugged me, because she didn't, but she did start to show some concern for me. On my sixteenth birthday, instead of 'passing' me a present, she actually gave it to me and wished me a Happy Birthday. I remember how nice it felt to have a present wrapped with a bow. I suppose I was more taken aback by that than the present, although the signet ring was lovely, and to this day I still wear it, the paper and bow meant so much more. Perhaps that is why, when I give a present, I take time to wrap it with a bow or ornament, to make it look special.

The factory closed again for its annual shutdown, and we were on the farm for the summer holidays. By now, Mum knew about my friendship with Trevor but wasn't very keen about me spending time with him. In the end, she conceded defeat, realising opposition would only cause conflict and upset. At the time, Dad wasn't in the best of health, and we hoped some good country air would do his chest the world of good and any upset would only aggravate his condition. He hadn't wanted to come to the farm, I suppose it was the thought of a six-hour journey, but nevertheless, he started to enjoy it.

Most evenings, Trevor and I would meet in the club, chatting together. I still found making conversation difficult, although spending time at the club was helping with my confidence. On one occasion, we went out as a foursome with a friend of Trevor's and his girlfriend. Although I found this challenging, we had a good evening as I was under no pressure to make conversation, with both Trevor and his friend doing most of the talking. Trevor was playing in a tournament at the Runt in Tun, a pub that was ten miles from Cross in Hand, and when he asked me if I would like to go with him, I said yes.

At the Runt in Tun Trevor won his darts match; we had a few drinks and chatted with some of his friends and other match players. I actually found the evening enjoyable; everyone was very friendly and conversation flowed easily. The match finished at 9.00 o'clock and Trevor suggested we stop and have fish and chips on the way back to the club as he had promised Auntie I would be back no later than 11.00 o'clock.

We sat in the car and ate out of the paper, washing the food down with cans of pop. Trevor suddenly asked me if I had ever seen a blue movie. Shocked that he had even asked that sort of question, it took me a few seconds to answer, "No, I haven't; why do you ask?" He explained that some friends of his were having a few people around that night to watch some movies and would I like to go. To this day, I will never understand why I said yes. The Only explanation I have is one of teenage inquisitiveness. It was something I'd never seen or even thought about before, and I suppose it roused my curiosity. That is not meant as an excuse, but it's adolescence, and let's face it, we all go through it.

We arrived at the house just after half past nine. There were about ten people there, none of which I had met before, and I immediately felt intimidated by the situation I found myself in. I should have been honest with Trevor straight away, but I settled down with him to watch the film. Within fifteen minutes, I had seen enough and walked out with Trevor following fast on my heels. When he asked me what was wrong, I burst into tears and couldn't stop. We sat in his car and he held me until I'd finished crying, saying how sorry he was and thought it would be a laugh; he hadn't meant to upset me.

I let Trevor think the film was the problem, but it wasn't the main reason I was upset. I found most of it revolting, but when a scene portrayed a situation very similar to one I had experienced with Matthew, I had to get out. It brought back to me the horror of what had happened, and how I had felt. But as I sobbed, I suddenly realised, this film had showed me Matthew was not the only man to enjoy this sort of behaviour. That in fact, men seemed to relish it, and there were obviously women who were willing to take part in this sort of performance. I would never judge any woman for the life she chooses, or the path taken, because you never know the circumstances behind their choices. But my heart breaks for any woman who finds herself in a situation where she has to do things she is not comfortable with. We should give these women every support we can to enable them to extricate themselves from these situations.

Once the tears subsided, Trevor drove me home to the farm, but I couldn't stop thinking about the film. I kept questioning why women allowed men to do such awful things to them. Was it normal? Perhaps there is nothing wrong, in which case, why do I feel so ashamed, dirty and mentally tormented by Matthew's actions? I knew the women in the film did it for money, but how could they? Perhaps that's why Mum hadn't believed me when I told her about Matthew.

With so many thoughts going round in my mind, I didn't get much sleep that night, and the next day I felt tired and irritable. I didn't do much during the day except lying in the fields and letting the warm sun caress my body until I finally fell asleep.

Trevor and I met regularly during the holiday. Bearing in mind I was only fifteen, Mum wasn't best pleased, but it was tough as far as I was concerned. I still had a problem making friends and looked at Trevor as someone who made me laugh, treated me well, and showed me respect. I'm not sure how it happened, but we started going out as a couple. Looking back, it was no different than it had been before we were dating. We didn't kiss and go sloppy over each other, but at times we did hold hands, which I liked as it made me feel safe, but I didn't want anything else.

All was fine until one particular night. We had gone to another darts match, this time at the Cow and Goat in Maresfield about forty-five minutes away, which was a lovely run out through the country lanes. The darts team had a successful evening and were now in the semi-finals.

It must have been getting on for ten thirty when we decided it was time to go home. We had been travelling for around fifteen minutes, when Trevor pulled onto the verge and said "I've got to have a pee, back in a minute". On his return, he didn't restart the engine but asked for a kiss.

We had never kissed before, but I agreed, although it was not what I wanted. It was not that I didn't want to be kissed; I wanted to be kissed by a woman, not a man. The kiss started tenderly, and I even began to find myself enjoying it. Trevor explored, running his tongue around my lips and slipping it into my mouth. I didn't realise the significance of his kissing, but it became more forceful. He started to fondle my breasts and to rub his hands up and down my neck. His hands were on my legs, and I felt him pushing my skirt up, slipping his hand under my panties, and touching me. I pulled back and I told him, "No," and I meant it, but he wasn't taking any notice. My mind went into overdrive; I was silently screaming out to stop this and get away. In the dark, unexplored cavities of my mind, I heard my son's cry. It was a harsh reminder of what happened the last time I had been with a man. I sobbed for him to stop, but he climbed on top of me and pulled my panties down. He was strong, stronger than me, and as I felt him go inside me and his urgency, I knew again the shame of being used and abused by someone I had no control over. Once he was satiated, he withdrew from me, and suddenly realising what had happened, he started weeping and saying how sorry he was.

I sat for what seemed ages deep in my own thoughts, and at the same time listening to Trevor sobbing and repeatedly saying "Sorry, I'm so sorry, please, please forgive me." I am sure he was sorry, but he still had sex with me even though I had said no. I felt so ashamed I had allowed this situation to occur. Perhaps in some way, I had encouraged him or made him think it was ok to take advantage of me. First Matthew and now Trevor; two men who thought they could abuse me in the most vile and intimate way. I asked Trevor to take me home, and we travelled back to the farm in silence. I got out of the car, and not saying a word or looking back, I went into the house.

Even though Trevor kept phoning the farm to speak to me, I did not see him again during the rest of the holiday. Mum, of course, was pleased that our friendship had ended, but she had no idea why, and I wasn't about to tell her.

On returning home, a letter would arrive from Trevor almost every day, each one repeating how sorry he was and asking for forgiveness. I never replied to any of his letters, as I did not know what to say. How could I forgive him? As time passed, and I missed my period, I realised I was pregnant – how could I put that in a letter? But I knew I had to deal with this and so decided I would have to go to Sussex.

I had to make an excuse for wanting to return to the farm, and so I told Mum I was feeling really low and depressed and needed some time to recover. Mum gave me a lecture about giving up work, but she could see my mind was made up, and so with Auntie's agreement, I travelled down to Sussex and was met by Norma at the bus station. When she quizzed me about how long I would be staying, I was vague, saying I just needed some rest and hoped they were all right with me coming down, which of course they were, "You know you can stay as long as you like."

As I arrived on Saturday, I thought it better to wait until Monday before contacting Trevor. In the meantime, however, Auntie saw Trevor and mentioned I had come to stay for a while. Before Saturday night was over, Trevor phoned the farm and asked to speak to me. He started saying how sorry he was about what had happened, and he needed to talk to me and try to put things right between us. I agreed that we had a lot to discuss, and we could meet on Monday. He said he was banger racing on Sunday, but perhaps we could meet later that evening. As I needed time to think and prepare myself, I said I would rather wait until Monday, so it was agreed we would meet Monday evening.

Sunday evening came, and Auntie was ready as usual for her shift at the club. I decided to go with her because I knew Trevor wouldn't be there. During the last three months, I hadn't been sure if I should tell Trevor about the baby, but now my mind was clear, and I just wanted Sunday night to prepare myself. I don't think I would have come to this decision if it hadn't been for the letters from Trevor saying how sorry he was. Although I never replied to any of them, he never gave up writing, so I felt he had a right to know that he was going to become a father.

I didn't want this baby. I felt guilty for being pregnant again, and that somewhere in this big wide world was my son, the baby I wanted. The baby I still cry and yearn for so desperately it burns into my soul. The baby I was carrying now could not compare with the bond of love that I felt for my son, who I had never seen, but only heard. I really didn't know what to do or who to speak to. My only option was to talk to Trevor, and hope he would help me sort this mess out.

I'd been in the club about an hour when I saw a friend of Trevor's come in. He was an older man, probably around forty. He walked up to the bar and I took no more notice, until I heard him say to my auntie that there had been a terrible accident at the Hot Rod meeting that afternoon. He started to explain what had happened, and as he did, he became very emotional and stumbled out that one of the casualties was in fact Trevor. Before I could manage to get to the bar, he said that Trevor's injuries were fatal.

Everyone in the club knew Trevor and couldn't believe what they heard. I don't think it hit me until later that evening. Of course, I was dreadfully upset;

I had begun to see Trevor as a friend and was growing quite fond of him. He would have been the father of my unborn baby, and I had hoped he would help me through this mess I found myself in. My concerns now, perhaps selfishly, were for myself and how I would cope. He had literally left me holding the baby.

I couldn't process the reality of Trevor's death for a couple of days. It was like a bad joke, and any minute he'd pop his head around the corner, but that would never happen. As I came to terms with his death, I began to feel angry and cheated by him. I blamed myself for not talking to him sooner and blamed him for making me pregnant and then dying. Trevor was the only person I had felt comfortable with, and I knew he was sorry for what he had done. I was sure together, we would have been able to sort things out, but now I didn't know what I was going to do. The funeral was two days away, but I had already decided I wouldn't attend. I didn't know Trevor's family, and I most certainly would not tell them about the pregnancy. I had no room for grief in my emotions; I had too much on my mind.

Looking back, I was preoccupied with finding a solution to my life. Within two years, I'd managed, through my mixed-up adolescent actions, to find myself pregnant again. The pain of losing my son and the shame of the abuse I had suffered from Matthew were still on my mind. The only way to manage was to harden my heart, which had left me selfish, uncaring, and blind to the needs of others. I could not see that others were not entirely to blame, and perhaps, in some cases, I should look at my actions. At the time, the death of Trevor was more of an inconvenience than the sad event it undoubtedly was.

The hardening in my character changed me, as it was not my true nature. I showed no emotions other than being cold and aloof, which could be considered rude and uncaring. The more I built this protective wall around me, the higher I wanted it to be, and like an addiction I kept on building, until eventually it became my enemy controlling my life and preventing me from trusting anyone.

With Trevor's funeral over, I felt no regrets for not going. In fact, I felt a complete detachment from his memory. In a week, I'd gone from not believing he'd died to erasing any part of our friendship from my mind. I'd even denied that Trevor played any part in my pregnancy. As far as I was concerned, it was my baby, my problem. I couldn't say I felt on my own because I was used to that feeling; it was my second nature. I was unsure where my life was going, but this time I was older, and one thing was certain, whatever decision was made, this time it would be mine and not my mothers.

CHAPTER FIVE

I desperately wanted the sanctuary of my own bedroom at home, but that meant being in my mother's company and control again. I hated the thought of that; I knew if I went home, Mum would start quizzing me about my time at the farm. I hadn't decided about the baby I was carrying, but I knew I was running out of time. I felt it would be better to stay at my aunties until I was sure what I wanted and had found the strength to stand by my decision.

I sort companionship and answers from my friend, the stream, but as in previous visits, it no longer held the answers I needed. I cannot say I didn't still feel peace when I was by the stream, but it no longer connected with me in the same way. Perhaps it was because I was older, and my innocent perception of things had changed. I knew it wouldn't give me an answer to my problem, that was something I had to work out for myself, but at least the stream gave me the peace and quiet to think.

By now, I'd been at the farm for almost two weeks. I spent many hours at the stream contemplating my decision and realising I had three choices. I knew in my heart from the moment I realised I was pregnant I didn't want to keep the baby. I felt no love, commitment or even bonding. The only genuine emotion was one of resentment and anger towards something that was growing inside me. I hated how it confused my mind, resulting in a battle between my heart and head. I'd entered a jungle of my own making, one of predator and survivor.

As a survivor, which was no strange phenomenon to me, I only had my heart to guide me in the right direction. Although I had built a brick exterior and which made me cold and calculated, I wondered if my heart was the wisest choice to follow. There was, however, one thing that made me weak, and that was the love for my son. I yearned for him every day and felt so guilty for carrying another child. I had cheated my son out of being with his natural mother and wasn't about to cheat on him again.

I wondered who or what really was in control of this situation. My heart that couldn't see any love other than for my son, or my head controlled by an unborn child that had turned into a predator.

My heart wanted me to lose this baby, and I begged God to rid me of it and give me back my son. But instantly, I could not believe I wanted something killed and felt guilty for having these thoughts. I felt as though my heart was telling me that even if I kept this baby, I would never be a mother to it; that I would always resent it and probably treat it the same way my mother treated me, and that was not what I wanted for any child.

I really could not understand why I felt so much resentment for this innocent unborn child. Was it because of the love and guilt I felt for my son? Or was I worried I would have to give up another child? Or was it the apprehension that I may be allowed to keep this baby? I knew if that were the case, the guilt of having to give up my son would only deepen and undoubtedly affect my relationship with this unborn child.

I selfishly wanted a future, although I was not sure what that life would be like. All I knew, I needed someone to love me, and probably my unborn child would, but what if I couldn't love it in return, and worst still repeat the inevitable hatred between Mother and child, as was the case of my Mother and me. Although I still hadn't decided, it had become clearer why I didn't want this baby.

I remembered I had heard in certain circumstances Doctors can perform terminations of pregnancies. Perhaps that's what I should do, but how and where would I go to find out and more to the point, would they do it? I began to get excited to think at last I'd found an answer, but the more I thought about the idea, the more unrealistic it became. I realised to do this I needed help, and the only person I could think of was Norma, but that wouldn't be any good as Norma was both my cousin and Godmother; she would have to tell Mum, and she was the last person I wanted to know. Unfortunately, this brought me back to square one again, with nowhere to turn.

I knew when I told Mum I was pregnant again she would be furious, and like before, she would show no compassion or support. I wasn't about to tell her the circumstances and so I would just have to accept the inevitable punishment of having the baby taken away from me. Although I didn't want this baby, I was not sure how I would feel when it was born. Would I have the same feelings I had for my son? Could I go through that loss again, having my heart torn in half as I listen to the cries as it is taken away from me.

But I knew my only choice was to tell Mum and accept the inevitable adoption. There was no way Mum would ever allow me to keep the baby, even if I wanted to.

At least I had come to a conclusion, and although I had to face telling Mum, I could allow myself a few days to enjoy the countryside and build up my courage. It must have been three or four days later, I decided to take a gentle walk across one of the fields. I'd nearly reached the pond at the far corner, when suddenly I started to feel a sensation of wetting myself. I realised it wasn't urine as I had first thought, but in fact it was blood. During the past few months, I had started to suffer from haemorrhoids, and they bled at times and so that's what I suspected this was, although they had never bled this much. It never crossed my mind that I may be losing my baby.

With the amount of blood that I seemed to be losing, I became concerned and decided to return to the farmhouse. I was almost back at the farm when I saw Norma in the garden. When she caught sight of me, she called to ask if I wanted to go shopping with her. I shouted back asking her to wait as there was something wrong. By the time I'd made it to the gate, Norma just looked at me and said, "What's wrong you are white as a sheet". While walking across the yard and into the house, I tried to explain what I thought was happening. She immediately understood because uncle also suffered from haemorrhoids, but this was too extreme. When she saw the amount of blood I'd lost, she decided to take me straight to the hospital.

Once inside the accident and emergency unit, we were settled in a cubicle and told a doctor would be with us shortly. For the first few minutes the waiting didn't seem too bad. Norma was there with me, and I could deal with my anxiety. However, as time continued to pass and we still hadn't seen the doctor, my mind started to conjure up all sorts of things. I began to wonder if this was God's judgement, and in fact whether he was about to make me suffer, even let me die for wishing ill of my unborn baby. I grabbed Norma's hand and told her I was frightened, but before I had a chance to tell her the truth about being pregnant, two people came into the cubical.

Norma rose from her seat. I thought she said "I will see you later" but wasn't sure as she disappeared behind the curtain. In a state of confusion and fear, my attention moved to a person dressed in white who was now coming towards me. I tried to focus through the mist of tears.

I was confused and scared; all I could see was someone standing beside me. In a state of delirium, I was convinced I was about to die, and this was God calling me to him. My fear turned to panic and although I desperately wanted to leave, I found I couldn't move. My feeble attempt to call out was nothing more than a mumble, and I felt as though I had lost the feeling in my arms and legs. My heart was racing and my whole body seemed to be closing down. Was this really the end? Was I about to die, alone and frightened? Death was surely not meant to be like this. And then I could hear a voice, my voice saying, "Please don't let me die". As I listened my voice became stronger, and then I felt someone take my hand and say, "You are not going to die, calm down and breath". She told me everything would be alright. Slowly my heart rate slowed and my mind calmed. I began to focus on the face of the Nurse and listen to what she was saying, realising that I was very much alive.

As I returned to reality, the Doctor examined me, asking me all the usual questions. Then he came to the one question I should have been prepared for, but I wasn't; did I know I was pregnant? There was no point lying, so I admitted that I knew.

The Doctor explained that the bleeding wasn't due to haemorrhoids, but that I was in fact starting to miscarry. He continued to say that I'd have to be admitted and have an operation, in his words, to clean me out. I wasn't altogether sure of this procedure, but as he told me that I'd be asleep and when I woke up it would all be over, I took him at his word. Before he left he asked if I had any questions or concerns, but really, I had none about the operation. However, I was worried that my family had to learn the truth and asked him whether this would be the case. Praying that his answer would be no, he agreed they did not have to know if that was my wish but did point out that some explanation would have to be given and he would sort it out.

After the Doctor and Nurse had left the room, it was several minutes before Norma came in to see me. I could tell she had been crying because of the state of her eyes, and that silly smile that she always did in an attempt to disguise her emotions and embarrassment. She asked how I was feeling, and I replied, I was fine and not to worry. I asked what the Doctor had said. "Not much", she replied and continued to say how frightened she had been for me, and had telephoned Mum. At this my heart went into my mouth and two thoughts came rushing into my mind. What the Doctor actually said to Norma, and why did she have to tell

Mum. Norma answered the questions in reverse order. She said that Mum had the right to know and that she would telephone her again later to keep her informed of my progress. She told me that Mum had to look after Dad so she couldn't come down, but as I didn't want her there anyway, it did me a favour. Finally I got to hear what the doctor had told Norma, and as he had promised he didn't tell the exact truth, but somehow skirted around it. He admitted to Norma that I had had a miscarriage but put the reason down to a phantom pregnancy. Norma obviously questioned his remark but after the doctor pointed out that it's just the same for animals, she accepted it. I can't tell you how relieved I was to hear that news and from then I relaxed and thanked God.

Lying in bed on the ward, waiting my turn to go to the theatre, I frankly couldn't have felt better. Mum was none the wiser, and I was no longer pregnant without having to make the most difficult decision about the baby. I felt almost euphoric, as though a great weight had been lifted from me, and now I was able to get on with my life. I didn't feel any sadness, a twinge of guilt or even anger, just sheer relief. I knew I would have found it impossible to have a termination, but at the same time, the thought of having another baby taken away from me was unbearable.

Once back from theatre and the anaesthetic had worn off, I had time to contemplate my life and what would become of me. I wondered if, when I was older and settled in life, I would by choice become pregnant. And in different circumstances, I would have children of my own; but did I really want to get married and would I ever get over the adoption of my son?

The answer to this lay deep within my heart, but I was too young and inexperienced to answer it. I was after all, still a child myself, although I felt as though I had an adult head sitting on my shoulders. The one thing I did know was that my life needed to change to allow me to live the life I should be enjoying as a fifteen-year-old.

I felt as though I had lost my childhood years ago, altogether that is strictly not true, in fact, I never had a childhood. As for my teens, they certainly were not spent as a teenager should. I had always found it difficult to make friends, not helped by the disruption to my life of constantly moving and never setting down roots. The decision I made years ago not be make friends, had to some extent protected me. But the result was I had become hard and isolated. Taking the option to use "identity formation" to escape my suffering, I had put a wall around me to keep the hurt and pain out, but it left me emotionally scared, which I did not recognise until years later. I had become the "iron child", showing no emotion, with an external hard shell to protect me that no-one could penetrate, but that's how I liked it. The only person I allowed in was Dad; the one person I loved, and I knew loved me back unconditionally.

The minute I was discharged from the hospital I knew I would have to return home, back to work and, if I was not careful, I would fall back into the old routine. I needed to save money so that when I was eighteen, I could move out and have my own place, away from control of Mum. To help me achieve my goals I would need Dad's help with my reading, writing and arithmetic, which I knew he would willing give. I only hoped Mum would not expect me to pay more housekeeping than I was currently paying, as that would seriously undermine my ability to save. It felt good; I had a plan and I felt positive and was determined nothing would stand in my way. All I needed now was all clear from the hospital so that I could be discharged.

It seemed I was waiting hours for the doctor to come and see me, but about two hours later he finally arrived, accompanied by a Sister. His face expressionless, he sat at the bottom of the bed and asked questions about how I was feeling. I said I was alright but a little tired. He began to explain about the surgical procedure that had taken place. Although, he said, the procedure is normally quite straight forward in my case there were a few complications. He continued, "As far as your miscarriage was concerned, we have dealt with that and everything is fine, but we have found numerous lumps called fibroids".

"As a general rule", he explained, "this usually occurs in much older women and although rare it does happen in people your age. We have managed to remove them all, but this does leave me having to tell you some rather upsetting news on two accounts. Firstly, these lumps, fibroids, are not dangerous but they may return, this however is no problem as they are simply removed again if necessary. This leads me to the second problem, unfortunately, not only did you have fibroids, but you also have a very thin lining to your uterus. Now this can either be due to the fibroids or the fact that its parts of your make up, whichever it is doesn't alter the fact that it is very unlikely that you will ever become pregnant again, but if you do later in life the chances are you will abort during the first three months". At this point, he asked if understood what he was saying and although he knew I didn't wish my family to be involved, he thought perhaps they should be so they could help me and give me moral support. I repeated that I did not want my family involved and I understood everything that he was saying, but it did not alter the fact that it was my body, and my wish was that only I knew. He was against my decision, but agreed to my request.

I understood all too well the odds of becoming pregnant again were low, and if I did, I would probably lose the baby. But this information didn't bother me, in fact I was grateful. Although I was determined this situation would never arise again, there was always an outside chance it could have done. Most women would have been devastated at the news, but I looked upon it as my saviour. I was just relieved to think this was another way of becoming even harder and untouchable, so that I would never have to make a heart wrenching decision again. In my mind it couldn't have worked out any better.

Some ten days later I was finally discharged from Eastbourne hospital, and I returned home, where I had no sympathy from my mother but thankfully I did from Dad.

The hospital, before I left, informed me that they would be witing to my own GP and I should make an appointment to see him in about two weeks' time. This was fine and I had no anxiety about going to see the Doctor, but I was concerned about doctor patient confidentiality. I felt sure the minute Doctor Vincent saw my mother, he would tell her everything. Doctor Vincent and his wife were both old school and believed parents should know everything about their son or daughter until they married. They also lived just two hundred yards away and knew my parents both personally, and as patients!

I made an appointment, and as luck would have it, neither Mum nor Dad had to see him in the intervening two weeks. On the day of the appointment, I found out exactly what the hospital had said, and then had to convince him why I didn't want Mum to know the truth. Doctor Vincent asked why Mum should not be told, and momentarily I wasn't sure what reason to give. I doubted he would have believed the truth about how Mum treated me, how she felt about me, and more to the point, how I felt about her. Doctor Vincent respected Mum, but that was the person she portrayed to outsiders; he didn't know the other side to her which was complicated and personal. The reason I used was one of Doctor Patient confidentiality, and that I was old enough to expect that from him. He disagreed with me, and tried to point out that my Mother had a right to know, after all he said, "She is your Mother". I tried to explain how cold Mum was towards me and how she had given my son up for adoption when I had wanted to keep him. At this point he interrupted in his stern and abrupt manner, saying Mum hadn't a choice because of Dad's illness. To some degree I could see his point, but it didn't alter how I felt about her or the situation I was in.

He suggested Mum could help me through this, and I should know that she felt guilty about the adoption, but under the circumstances that had been the only option. He imagined this could be a start to putting things right between us. His arrogant manner angered me, as he had no idea how my mother really was.

I decided to retaliate in the only way I knew how. I just looked at him and called him a stupid old fool who hadn't a clue. "You don't know my mother like I do, you don't know half the things that go on, and as for having any feelings, I doubt she has one ounce of compassion in her entire body and is never likely to". He kept trying to interrupt me, but I wouldn't have it. I wasn't sure whether I'd suddenly grown up and found I had a tongue in my mouth; whether I was frightened of Mum or if I had just had enough. Whatever the reason, I certainly wasn't frightened of Doctor Vincent and pointed out that the only people who knew the real truth were the hospital, myself and him, and if Mum should ever find out then I would know where it had come from, and I would have no hesitation in reporting him to the authorities. I can now hardly believe the arrogance of a fifteen-year-old!

I was so angry when I left the surgery and walked outside into the fresh air. I stood there for a while just trying to catch my breath and come down from the burst of adrenaline. I couldn't believe where my strength had come from. Part of me was proud of myself, but on the other hand I was ashamed of my behaviour. For a moment I wanted to walk back into the surgery and apologise for my rudeness, but then again, why should I? After all he wasn't on my side, that was perfectly clear. If anything, it only proved a valuable lesson that I couldn't even trust my own Doctor.

As I walked away from the surgery towards the bus station, I wondered if Doctor Vincent would risk me reporting him, or whether he would think it was just an idle threat on my behalf. More to the point, I wondered if it did go that far would the authorities believe me anyway. Fortunately, it never came to that, as I am confident Mum never found out the truth, if she had, I'm sure I would have felt the tidal wave!

From that day I noticed a change in my attitude. My concentration and my get up and go diminished so rapidly that I hardly recognised myself. Glimpses of the past flashed across my mind and then disappeared. Not one thought would stay long enough for me to recall every detail. A bit like a dream you can't quite remember, it was there one minute and gone the next.

After a time my work began to suffer, and I started making stupid mistakes which meant starting at the beginning again. I was losing money hand over fist, and it came to a point where my wages had dropped by half. My home studying with Dad had also taken a dive, and I felt I was going backwards instead of forwards. If this wasn't bad enough, I had started to lose my drive to achieve the goals I had set myself; I wondered why, not fully appreciating how the trauma of the last few months had affected me.

I became obsessed with finding the reason why this was happening, but at the same time, I wanted to be free, and not be continually worrying about the road my life was taking. I was still in my teens and should be enjoying life, but I felt I was being taken over by something that didn't make sense. I kept having flashbacks, which included the hatred that I felt towards my mother, to the love that I felt towards my Dad. From the relief I felt about the loss of my baby, to the grief of having my son taken from me for adoption; to the events that happened in the shed and the sadness of losing my Gran. The more I tried to concentrate on my life, the more I found it to be increasingly impossible.

Never being free of the past meant thoughts continually went around in my mind, and two dominated my existence. Firstly, the one I could understand and was constantly ripping me apart, was not having my son. Each day my heart broke a little more, but all I could do was hope with time, it would become easier to live with. Knowing nothing could be done to change the situation, and learning to accept it, maybe would reduce the heartbreak; but to be frank, I didn't believe anything could take away the pain I was feeling.

Although every day I missed him, and the recent events had only enhanced my yearning for him, this wasn't the only mental upset that I was plagued with. The second issue was a loss of my 3-month-old pregnancy. I could not understand why I felt such a sense of loss for a baby I didn't want to have. I should be feeling relief having had a miscarriage, but there was something I couldn't get to grips with, and it tormented my mind so that I couldn't think of anything else. It wasn't anything definitive, it was just there, a nagging sense of loss, and I didn't know why. My waking hours were bombarded with these thoughts, and I was tormented and frustrated by not being able to process or understand my emotions.

All I knew was that my son was alive, and I grieved his loss every day; the other baby was dead, and even though I had not wanted the pregnancy, I was feeling a sense of bereavement. These two issues were tormenting me so much, I was losing my grip on everything around me.

I finally arrived at a state of mental exhaustion and didn't know what to do or even where to turn.

I knew I needed help, whether this was medically or psychologically I wasn't sure, but I knew that I couldn't continue to go on if I wasn't to have a complete breakdown. I wondered whether I should go and see Doctor Vincent, but on reflection I knew what his attitude would be towards me, and instead of helping me he would have given me a lecture saying, "The last time I saw you, you considered yourself old enough to make your own decisions and wouldn't take my advice, so I recommend you pull yourself together and act the age that you think you are."

Obviously I couldn't take the chance with Doctor Vincent and I doubted that I could have looked him in the face after what happened the last time I saw him, besides, I hadn't got any confidence in him as a doctor. I did, however, consider telling Mum the truth and hoped what Doctor Vincent had said about Mum feeling guilty would be true. I needed someone to talk to before I went crazy, but could I trust Mum? Could I really trust the person that hurt me so much, a person that had treated me like a door mat for so long? Could I risk opening my heart to this woman only to have it thrown back in the face, with the result of once more becoming open and vulnerable to her tormenting? No, I couldn't allow myself to be that foolish and stupid. Whatever was wrong with me it was something that I and only I could solve. For a moment I had become weak or was it just the case I wished I had a mother like everyone else had, who you could trust and talk to; perhaps that's what it was.

I thought of the plan I'd made in hospital and instantly the words, "Don't trust anyone," came into my mind. Whatever was wrong with me, whatever was going on in my head, it was up to me to solve and no one else. I decided to keep my mouth shut and trust no one, and I would manage to overcome this problem.

Although having accepted I had to resolve these issues myself, I still felt confused and emotionally exhausted. I kept wondering how my little boy was doing; was he happy? Was he being well looked after and loved? And what about the baby I had lost; was it a girl or a boy? Had it suffered during the miscarriage? I relived the birth of my son and being taken away from me immediately after, and the miscarriage, which had been a relief at the time, but was now inflicting me with guilt. I kept having these flashbacks, until I was mentally exhausted.

One evening I had gone to bed as usual about ten pm and could hear Dad snoring in the other bedroom. Mum had gone next door for her usual chat with Matthew, which, over the years had become a routine that never faltered. The thought that she wanted to associate with that dirty pig still amazed and hurt me and showed exactly where her loyalties lay. I had been in bed about an hour and was getting fed up with tossing and turning, so I decided to get up for a drink of water and a tablet as my head was throbbing, which was not unusual. After returning to bed I finally settled down and the tablet started to work. For a while I drifted in and out of a sleepy state, when suddenly I heard a noise, no not a noise but a voice. I heard it again and then another one, but it wasn't like a normal voice and although muffled, it sounded more like two young children. I couldn't quite make out what they were saying until their voices began to get stronger and clearer.

Now it was as if they were talking directly to me, but it didn't make any sense what they were saying.

In a state of half sleep, I heard them say "Do you know who we are?" "We could give you a clue and tell you that you are our mother". Shocked, I told them, "I don't know what you mean, and any case I'm not a mother in the real sense of the word, but I did give birth to my son." "Yes, that's right, I'm your son, but you didn't want to keep me, did you? So you gave me away" "No" I said, "I didn't, it wasn't like that, believe me I wanted to keep you." "What about me then"? the other little voice shouted; "You didn't want me at all did you"? "Who are you?" I asked. "Don't you know, you should do, I'm the baby that you killed, you know the daughter you didn't want, remember now?" "I don't know what you're talking about, I haven't got a daughter, only a son". "Yes that's right you gave him away didn't you, but at least he was allowed to live, I wasn't and I'll never forgive you for that". "I loved my son" I shouted angrily "and I was so sorry and still am, but I didn't have any choice if I had I would surely have kept him, and God knows how desperately I wanted to". "I know" interrupted my son, "I realise that now, I didn't mean to hurt you forgive me please and don't worry because one day we will meet, don't feel sad anymore, it's alright". "It's alright, it's alright" screamed a high-pitched voice "is that all you can say, it's alright; what about me, why didn't you want to love me, tell me what I had done so wrong". "She hadn't done anything wrong" answered my son, "it wasn't you. You see she was so hurt about my adoption that she couldn't think or feel for another baby. She couldn't see that it wouldn't make any difference to me, she didn't realise that I wasn't a selfish person, but somehow, she felt that she was letting me down if she had you and if anything, she didn't want to let me down for the second time. You have got to forgive her. You'll never get another chance". A little voice, this time not as loud asked me to forgive her. I didn't answer, but then the voice said again, "Will you forgive me Mum"? Angrily I shouted out "Don't call me that, I'm not your mother". "No and you're not likely to be now after you destroyed me, and you are never likely to be a mother again are you.? You can't have any more children, can you? I only wanted to be loved by you, that's all, surely that wasn't too much to ask. I wanted the same as you wanted, love from a mother but you know how it feels not to receive any, don't you? Please don't let me continue in my death knowing that you have no love for me, please don't make me suffer anymore. I have one chance at peace and only you can help me. Look deep into your heart and find me. Please help me Mum, so that I can help you. Don't you see, we are both in our own worlds of torment and if we don't settle this now, we are going to be two very lonely lost souls without any hope."

Suddenly before my eyes, I saw an image of a beautiful baby lying in a crib. Her eyes, I noticed, were like looking at my own reflection, but there was one big difference, these were loving caring eyes and not cold as stone like mine. I heard a voice again, and although it didn't appear to be coming from the baby's mouth, I recognised it as the voice that had been telling me that she was my daughter. The voice asked me to hear what she had to say.

"From the moment I was conceived" she said, "I started to develop and had a life in my own protective world that you had unwillingly provided. As time progressed and with me becoming stronger each day, I began to feel the pain and anguish that you were suffering. It was bad enough to know that you didn't love me and all you wanted was your son, which would have been my half-brother. I wasn't there to take his place, but to be your daughter and another person in my own right. Your thoughts, emotions, even your movements affected me with such hurt I began to feel a stranger trapped within alien surrounding. I was to you an object of hatred that you didn't want, and desperately wanted dead. I cannot deny I was angry and hurt by you, but I now understand the pain and upset you have suffered from your mother over the years, and how this affected your attitude towards me. I forgive you, and much more I love you. Look at me, I'm your daughter. You don't really hate me, do you? You've come this far to find me, forgive me as I forgive you, I beg you please."

With tears now turning into sobs and catching my breath, I started to search for something that I had convinced myself didn't exist. I looked in every corner of my heart and knew that I was running out of time. A pang of guilt and betrayal swept over me, and at the same time, a little voice asking me to hurry.

Desperate now, I started to move towards the baby, wanting so much to cradle her in my arms, but the closer I seemed to get to the baby, the more the image faded away. I panicked and shouted, "Don't go, please don't, you really are my baby daughter aren't you"?

I wanted to hold her and cry with her in my arms. "Please" I said again, "don't go. Forgive me, I'm so sorry, I do love you." I reached out, but the image like a candle that flickers at the end of its life, had faded completely and left darkness.

Through the profusion of tears, I cried as loud as I could, "Did you hear" I said, "answer me, did you hear me"? Panicking to hear an answer, because it was the same feeling as when my son was taken from the delivery ward. I suddenly realised how much she meant to me, and the emotions I was feeling were grief at her loss. I shouted again and this time she did answer. I could hardly hear what she was saying, she seemed so far away and slightly muffled. "I heard you Mum" she said, "thank you and I love you too". But then silence. "Are you still there?" I cried, but there was nothing but silence and emptiness surrounding me.

Pleading, sobbing and uncontrollably shaking, I realised I was alone in my bedroom. Trying to calm myself down I wondered if it had been a bad dream. or whether it was a vision. It was far too vivid to have been a dream; dreams don't make you feel like this and even if it had been, then surely, I'd still be in bed and not standing in the middle of the room. On the other hand, if I wasn't dreaming then it must have been real, but dead people don't come back, do they? What if they did? No, that didn't make sense, the image of the baby I saw was at least three-month-old, and not a three-month-old foetus. And my son was there, and he was alive wasn't he? I suddenly started to panic because I couldn't recall seeing him. Perhaps that's the reason for all this, perhaps he'd died, and this was the only way of telling me. Instantly I knew that wasn't the case and that my son was alive and well; the foetus I had carried and lost was this baby girl, and they had come to tell me they forgave me. Whatever had possessed me to be so cruel and wicked to want to lose my baby? If I had wanted her, truly wanted her, would she have lived? I thought the answer was all too obvious, and whether this had been a dream or real was of no consequence, I had to learn to live with the truth somehow.

How would I come to terms with the fact I was convinced I had lost my baby girl due to my own selfish feelings; I had been adamant I hated this baby growing inside me, and wanted to be rid of it, but of course, really I loved her and was now feeling the guilt and shame of those feelings. How would I ever rid myself of this nightmare feeling I had killed my baby girl.

I always thought I was a Christian, but how could I be having asked God to help me destroy my baby? My mind would not allow me to see the miscarriage for what it was, but rather I found I wanted to destroy myself in an endeavour to put right a terrible wrong. I had no one to talk to and confide in, so the thoughts kept going round and round in my head. There was no one to give me a different perspective and so I continued to torment myself day and night. When you have something like this, you have to learn to live with it, or at least I did. Not a day went by without me thinking of my baby girl and what might have been, and whether my son was happy in a loving family. I would find myself close to tears when I saw a mother with her baby, but felt I had no right to such emotions as I had given up my son and lost my daughter. I felt ashamed

I had not fought more to keep my son and questioned how I had allowed my mother to take control of his destination and how cruel it had been to take my baby away from me as soon as he was born so that I never even got to hold him. I know I was very young when I gave birth to him, but the pain of loss was no less than had I been older. Added to that was not knowing what had happened to him, and my mother refusing to ever mention him. It was as though he did not exist, but he did, and I am tormented every day by not knowing if he is well and happy.

CHAPTER SIX

I was now nineteen, and still confused about what had happened in my bedroom two years ago with my son and unborn daughter. Whatever it was, it had taken a considerable amount of strength and will power for me to remain in control of my life and my sanity. Guilt and anger still raged, but to survive I learnt different ways to control the emotions just enough so that I could function.

I had to treat both the birth of my son and the loss of my daughter as episodes in my life and try to consign them behind my brick wall to protect me from further heartbreak. I wondered how much more I could possibly take before my wall crumbled, then thought of all the people that had gone through far more than I had and wondered how they manage. Perhaps their brick wall is stronger than mine I thought, but my wall was strong, and I knew I would survive.

Dad hadn't altered at all in the previous two years and was much his old self. He still couldn't do much and providing he had his paper, the television to watch the horse racing and a cup of tea, which he always left about an hour before drinking, he was fine.

Mum on the other hand had changed and had mellowed over the years, but still had the capacity to challenge me. I thought I would have been used to her mood swings, but I wasn't. After all these years and as much as I'd tried not to let it, she still hurt me and as much as I tried to work her out, I couldn't.

Of course, I had also changed too. After my miscarriage I had been told by the Doctor it was unlikely I would be able to have children in the future. I had always had "an old head on young shoulders", and I was now more mature and could understand the significance of what the Doctor had told me, although at the time it had not unduly concerned me, I know felt bereft at the thought my body was no longer capable of bearing children. My only chance of being a mother had been taken away, and while I was beginning to understand why my mother had done what she did, I could not forgive her.

It was strange to think that in just under a year my teenage years would come to an end, and I would begin a new adventure exploring my twenties. I wondered what that decade had to offer me and whether it would be better than this one. My teens had not been a good time for me, and I just wanted them to end. I know for a lot of young people teenage years are a time to have fun, explore life, make friends, fall in love. But for me, they were years of self-doubt, in a place I neither understood nor had the experience to deal with. I found myself in situations I was ill equipped to deal with, making bad decisions which would influence the rest of my life.

My plan to leave home at eighteen hadn't happened, and to be frank, if it had, I doubt I would have coped. I tried to pull myself together and concentrate on working and earning money, and for quite a while that was all I could seem to manage. Mum for some reason didn't ask for a rise in housekeeping which surprised me, and allowed me to start saving again.

Matthew still lived in the converted shop, and he continued to cultivate the garden, producing vegetables for us to use during both summer and winter months. But Matthew didn't have much idea on how to grow things, and although he dug the garden and planted seeds, I couldn't help but have a sarcastic smile on my face when he had to ask Dad for guidance. I really did despise Matthew, and as the years passed I surprised myself at how the depth of the hatred I felt deepened. When you are abused at a young age by someone who you should have been able to trust, your youth and inexperience does not allow you to process all the feelings, and it becomes impossible to move on because you cannot forget and forgive. My mother had not believed me and so there had been no way of dealing with my abuse; I had no-one to talk to; there was no-one to help me analyse what had happened to me and guide me through how I should cope with it. I felt bitter and vindictive towards him, and no amount of self-analysis would change that.

I recall one Saturday morning I had been working in the garden and found Matthew's crucifix in one of the vegetable beds. He must have lost it and not noticed. I knew how much it meant to him because he had told me his mother had given it to him when he was quite young. It was unusual because it was a string of tiny beads with a gold crucifix hanging down. My first thought was to return it to its rightful owner, as would anyone, but this was quickly replaced by a feeling of spite. Maybe I would just throw it away so he would never find it and never know what had happened to it. But an even better idea came to mind.

Matthew had been out all morning and as soon as I heard the gate open, I went out to meet him. With a smile on my face, I asked him if he had lost his crucifix as I had found one in the garden opening my hand to show him the crucifix lying there. His face lit up as he recognised it but was curious when I snapped my hand shut, the smile gone from my face. Matthew, being Matthew, totally misread the situation and put his hand out to receive the crucifix thanking me for finding it, and telling me what a clever girl I was, how I must love him and how he would like to thank me in a special way. All these years later, and he still thought he could treat me like that. He kept smiling and telling me how grateful he was, thanking me for finding it. But the years had given me an inner strength, and I was now able to stand up to him and not feel intimidated. I stood tall, squared up to him and said, "You are nothing but a dirty old man, and I have no intention of giving it back to you." As I went to turn away, he said, "That belongs to me, and you return to me now." From the expression on his face, I instantly knew just how important this was to him. The smile had gone, replaced by an anger I had not seen before. But I was resolved to carry out my plan, and so as we stood looking at each other I took the crucifix in both hands and held it over the drain and snapped the thread allowing the beads to fall into the drain, followed by the crucifix. I thought he was going to explode, but he dropped to his knees, pulling the drain cover off and started groping amongst the grime and dirt to find the broken crucifix. This may have seemed sadistic and cruel, but I enjoyed watching him desperately searching and so obviously upset, I could see the tears in his eyes. I hoped he felt just a little of how I had felt when I was abused by him, and maybe the loss of something he clearly cherished would go some way to teaching him a lesson, although I had my doubts. This man had flirted with me as a friend when I was too young to understand the connotations of what he was doing. He took advantage of my innocence, secure in the knowledge that not only could he control me but also had the adoration of my mother so she would believe him over me every time. As I turned and left him looking for the crucifix, I threw back a comment, "An eye for an eye – but don't ever believe what are you experiencing compares with what you have done to me in the past." And with that I walked away.

During the past twelve months I had spent a lot of time thinking about my sexuality. My inner most feelings were telling me that I was gay, but I didn't know any gay people and had no idea how to go about meeting other women who shared my feelings. This was the 1970's when there was no social media, and the gay movement was only just beginning with the first London Pride taking place in March 1972. The thought of being affectionate with a women intrigued me. Sharing a life with someone who was on the same wavelength as me and who would not take advantage or abuse me.

My life so far had been isolated due to the constant moving and new schools, so I had not made friends and had no one to talk to about my feelings. I knew I could not confide in either Mum or Dad as this was still a taboo subject in most families, and my parents would certainly not have known how to deal with this. All I knew was that there was still a consensus that gay people were nothing but freaks of nature, abnormal, perverted, and to many a subject of ridicule and abuse. I was pretty sure if I told Mum how I was feeling, her reaction would be to tell me this was just a "phase" that would pass.

It was hard to imagine a feeling that was so strong and felt so natural, could be reviled and offensive to so many people. However, I could understand some of the objections, as my initial thoughts about same sex relationships was revulsion, especially the idea of two men together. But this was based on ignorance and was no grounds for the abuse and cruelty that was thrown at gay people by some sadistic individuals.

I'd been brought up to believe the "normal" was one man and one woman and when I started to question the gay movement, I found a society that was bigoted and ignorant, dogmatic in their opinions which often transpired into violence. From my first gay feelings, although shocking, I had found myself in an unknown world of gay hatred. This was a world that I really didn't wish to be involved with, and as society had already dictated it would never be accepted, I fought to stop my feelings.

But I struggled to suppress the very existence of my emotions. Now at the age of nineteen, I fully realised, that being gay wasn't my fault, in fact it wasn't anyone's fault. Time had made me understand that it wasn't a disease, it wasn't an illness I could recover from, it wasn't a trend, a phase that I was going through, it was something that I hadn't a choice over.

I tried so hard not to allow these feelings become the better of me, but I knew that one day I would meet someone, and these feelings would materialise into an emotional adventure. As I matured, it became harder to fight the desire to have a gay relationship, but it still felt wrong due to the attitudes in general of society and, those of my mother. I knew she would never understand or accept I was gay. My only choice was to put my efforts into some activity which would take my energies and stop me from continually thinking about my sexuality.

From a very early age I had been interested in anything medical and had always wanted to become a doctor. Unfortunately, this could only be a dream, my lack of education left me without a chance of ever achieving that goal. I had, however, some years ago, passed my first aid examination through the St Johns Ambulance Brigade. As this examination only involved a practical exam and not written, I managed to pass with ease. I was pleased as punch and so was my Dad. Bless him, he gave me ten shillings and told me how proud he was of me. I was so pleased, this recognition meant more to me than the certificate. The certificate was only valid for three years and after that a retest was required. I should have resat when I was fourteen, but with so many factors affecting my life at that time, I didn't have the inclination to undergo another exam, so did no more about it.

Five years on, and trying to find something to occupy my mind, I sat the examination not only for First Aid but also a basic Home Nursing Certificate and successfully passed both. At the same time, I also decided to enrol as a member of the St Johns Ambulance Brigade. My decision to enrol wasn't an easy one due to my lack of outward confidence and I wasn't under any illusion that joining would put me through a great deal of mental and physical pressure, but it was something that I knew I had to do. At nineteen I had no choice but to prove to myself that I could go out into the big wide world and stand on my own two feet.

The first night, although I was anxious, it proved not to be the worst, as the subsequent weeks were awful. I hated walking into the room which I only managed to do after standing outside for ten minutes or more, building up the courage to go in. I was so apprehensive probably due to shyness, embarrassment and fear of the unknown. Meeting new people and making conversation was still very difficult for me, and I would feel the nerves building up as I entered the room. As I shut the door, I felt everyone looking at me as the room hushed before conversations resumed. Someone would look up and say good evening, but all I could manage was a whisper, almost inaudible as my throat appeared to be paralysed. With beads of perspiration trickling down my back, I'd make a conscious effort to reduce the erratic beating heart and quickening breath, but as soon as someone spoke to me it returned with vengeance, making talking almost impossible and so I would end up sounding like a blithering idiot not able to string more than two words together. Bandages and dressings were laid out for that evening's practice, but all I wanted to do was run, to get outside and breath fresh air and never return. I'd look across the room towards the door and the sign marked exit, but it may as well have been a million miles away. The sickening feeling that seemed to involve every part of my body, the dry mouth, the feeling faint and of being out of control; I felt like a child that had been abandoned; no one can ever understand unless they had experienced these feelings for themselves.

Eventually I came to terms with these agonising panic attacks, which I am sure were due to past childhood experiences and events. I had overcome a great deal in my life so far, and I most certainly wasn't going to let a panic attack rule me, but at thirty-nine they still affect me, especially at times of stress, however by having a better understanding I have learnt to cope with them. They are unpleasant, but I believe that if you have faith in God and one's own strength and determination, you can beat the anxiety. I treated these panic attacks as an unseen coward, something that can't show its face yet tries to control your life, so deserves to be irradicated. Each time I experienced an attack, I visualised a faceless attacker bent on controlling me; I would rationalise my thoughts, controlling my breathing, until I realised that I was in control and slowly the attack dispersed into the ether.

Mum had been a little easier to live with, but still I needed my space away from her and with my decision to join the St Johns, although it was initially to occupy my mind, it gave me a freedom from her. However, this freedom proved to be short lived, as Mum decided to join three months later. I tried to explain that it was something that I wanted to do on my own, but she had made up her mind that she was going to join, and that was that.

Although angry with her at the time as I felt she was being selfish not to allow me my own space, as the weeks unfolded something between us surprisingly mellowed. As we were mother and daughter it was assumed that at the Monday night meeting we would practice on each other. So, we were forced together and because of that we were also placed in a position that we must be seen to be civil to each other. During the next few months, we attended track events and fetes together as St John's volunteers, and we both realised we had a mutual interest in something we were able to share. Surprisingly the ice started to melt between us at home, which made life much easier. Even so, it didn't mean that I trusted her, I'd never be able to do that, and as for the hurt she had caused me, that would never go away either. Knowingly or not, she had managed to damage our relationship for so long, that twice a lifetime couldn't build the bridges to eradicate the suffering she had put me through and I would never feel I could trust her as a daughter should be able to trust her mother.

Mum and I would never be the best of friends which saddens me. If only she had given me half a chance, I'm sure we would have made it. I really can't begin to explain what she put me through, its too painful to find the words. I always believed love to be a genuine and unconditional, but my mother's love was far from that. A child needs its Mother's tender love to feel safe and secure, and sadly I'll never know what that feels like.

But, as things between us seemed to be on a level footing, I could only hope that it would last and we would achieve a little respect for each other. We could never build love between us, that was an impossible task, but I hoped life could be a little more comfortable.

The person that helped me during my initial weeks at the St Johns was a man called Nigel. He was a member but came from the Evesham division. I later learnt the reason for him being at Redditch Division was solely to keep the number of members up, which by all accounts had dropped below the minimum requirement, resulting in a number of events which couldn't be covered, so the division was keen to attract new members.

I felt sure Nigel sensed my uneasiness, and through his kindness and thoughtfulness, helped me to overcome my anxiety. Within a few weeks I found that my nervousness had abated considerably, and when Nigel asked me out for a quite drink after the meeting, although initially I refused this kind invitation, after some persuasion, I eventually accepted.

The Monday night drinks gradually transpired into most evenings, until some months later, Nigel's mother invited me to stay Saturday night and return home after Sunday dinner. From the first stop over, it became a ritual that most weekends we would stay at his parents.

Somehow, I'd managed to fall into a routine which was not actually of my making, but at the time I was experiencing freedom, and didn't recognise what was occurring. Out of the blue, Nigel asked me to marry him. Although this came as quite a shock, I must admit my reply came as a bigger one and not the answer I was prepared for. Within minutes I'd answered "yes" but had no idea why. I'd accepted a proposal from a man that I hadn't known that long and bearing in mind my sexual preference and nature, I was either crazy or just very confused, I didn't know which.

Nigel had made it quite clear that he loved me and would be honoured to have me as his wife and sooner rather than later. Unfortunately, I didn't share the same kind of love for him. I enjoyed his company but as for love, I couldn't love him, I couldn't love any man for that matter, not in that way, but still I agreed to marry him.

Nigel was a nice man in his own way, inoffensive, and I really couldn't have found anyone kinder towards me. At the time marriage seemed my only option to a future which would be accepted by society and of course, my mother. It never occurred to me I could have a relationship with a woman, and we may be able to live together as a couple. I had no friends I could discuss my feelings with, and so this appeared to be my only choice. In my heart, I knew it was wrong, and that I could never be the wife that Nigel wanted or deserved.

Because I wasn't in love with him and didn't have the benefit of "love is blind", I soon began to see the other side of Nigel's character. His lack of knowledge about many things I knew about, and I would have expected him to know about too aggravated me. He portrayed himself as a bit of a jerk, without an opinion or conviction of his own. I began to recognise in him the dominance of a mother who managed his life and rendered him incapable of his own decisions. In fact, his relationship with his mother was very similar to mine and my mother. The only difference I could see was the fact he was a mummies boy, idolised by his mother and protected from the trials of growing up, and he was quite happy with this situation.

I look back now, and question why I agreed to marry him. I realise I used him as a means by which to gain freedom from my mothers' control. Knowing the person that I am now, I feel ashamed of my behaviour and truly sorry for my actions, but in hindsight I don't believe I fully understood what I was doing. That remark sounds like a get out statement, but honestly at the time I was a very mixed-up individual who wanted to be free from her mother's powerful control, and all I saw was an opportunity; I didn't see the hurt I would cause, or the consequences that my own turmoil would create.

The marriage took place on the twenty-first of December 1974. This was just under three months after our first meeting. My wedding dress wasn't a new one, handed down from my cousin Norma's wedding some fifteen years prior. The veil, however, was much older and belonged to my great grandmother which she wore at her wedding. The thought of wearing someone else's wedding dress didn't appeal to me, but on reflection, if I could look half as good as Norma had looked on her wedding day, I would be happy. Strangely enough the importance of how I looked on the day wasn't for Nigel, my future husband, but for my Dad and no one else. I so wanted him to be proud of me.

Mum had put a stop to who I had wanted as my Matron of Honour, saying that she didn't like Christine, and as she was paying for the wedding, then she should have some say in who the matron of honour was. Anyway, it was agreed I would ask Rachel. She was a girl I used to work with at the factory, until I was given promotion and worked as a training instructor in a different area. We didn't stop being friends because of that, but as she was six years older than me and had a boyfriend, we restricted our friendship to work only. Christine, who also worked at the factory and was my age, became a good friend, but unlike Rachel, our friendship materialised socially and I felt much closer to her than I ever did to Rachel. I think Christine was always surprised I had asked Rachael to be my Matron of Honor and not her, and I never did explain why, but her kind nature meant she never held a grudge.

Half an hour before we were due to leave for the church Rachel arrived. We consumed four double gin and tonics each and were about to start on the fifth when Mum came into the room. She probably played the best performance of her life and I felt embarrassed that she was acting as if she had the starring role. She came in all emotional and asked for a gin and tonic. Rachel quickly poured her one and of course poured us another one. Mum asked Rachel to raise her glass and drink my health and happiness for the future and then immediately gave me a kiss on the cheek. There was no hug, holding of hands, nothing other than a peck on the cheek, which felt so false, and I have no doubt it was, as it was so out of character for her to act in this way. Before she left the room, she gave me an old looking piece of paper. Mum told me that it was given to her on her wedding day by her mother and that now she had pleasure in giving it to me. It was obviously a delicate paper that was folded into four and I opened it with great care. Reading it, I was astonished at the content. I wanted to rip it up, burn it, even throw it back at her and tell her to eat the words as they meant nothing to me, but realised it wouldn't achieve anything.

The paper was in fact a poem entitled "We can only have one mother".

We can only have one mother,
Patient kind and true,
No other friend in the world,
Will be so true to you;
For all her loving kindness,
She asks nothing in return;

If all the world deserts you,
To mother you can turn.

Many tears you have caused her,
When you were sad or ill,
Maybe many sleepless nights,
Tho' you may cause her still.
So every time you leave her,
Or whenever you come and go,
Give her a kind word and kiss,
Tis what she craves I know.

We can only have one mother,
Non else can take her place.
You can't tell how you'll need her,
Till you miss her loving face,
Be careful how you answer her,
Choose every word you say,
Remember she's your mother
Tho now she's old and grey.

We can only have one mother,
So take her to your heart,
You cannot tell how soon the time,
When she and you will part,
Let her know you love her dearly,
Cheer and comfort her each day,
You can never get another,
When she has passed away.

By the time I had reached the end of the poem, I couldn't believe that she of all people had given something that under normal circumstances would have been treasured, but to this day I will never know whether she really meant it and it was a peace offering. I would like to think it was given with sincerity, but at the time I was extremely angry and could see nothing but her again playing her mental games. She had offended and hurt me to the extent all I wanted to do was throw it back in her face. It was then that I knew I was lucky to get away from her, and any reservations I had had about marrying Nigel were locked away.

I placed the poem to one side and immediately poured myself another stiff drink. I was surprised I wasn't drunk with the amount that I'd already consumed, especially as I really did not drink a great deal, but I suppose the tension of the day and the upset kept me sober.

Everyone except for Dad had already gone to the church. I'd had a few quite moments in my bedroom before Dad knocked at the door and asked if he could come in. It was only hearing his voice that I began to calm down. He entered the room and just stood there saying nothing. He remained perfectly still with just a tear or two as he looked at me. His face radiated love and gentle warmth that made me want to join him in his tears. I hadn't felt any emotion from Mum's actions, but with the love and respect I felt for my Dad I couldn't stop the tears flowing. By marrying Nigel I felt as though I was abandoning Dad and in a way I was; I felt I was leaving him to fight the battle of control my mother would undoubtedly turn on him when I had gone. Dad was a twelve stone man and before my very eyes, he seemed to be crumbling emotionally. His suit which I'd never seen him in before, fitted him perfectly and made him look extremely handsome and very distinguished. For a moment it was as if the only thing that existed, was him, me and our unspoken love. The car had arrived to take us to church, but it would have to wait, a nineteen year old girl and a sixty-seven year old man had something far more important than a wedding. We had always loved each other but the fact was always there that we were not related and this sadly left a trace of feeling incomplete. This, however, was different and for the rest of our lives we would feel this closeness that could never be broken, that we were completely father and daughter in every sense of the word.

This was the first time in a very long time we had been alone, I mean truly alone that we couldn't be interrupted; that Mum wouldn't walk in; the telephone ring; the telly on or someone may call. We were finally alone, and it was our special time together and I hoped that all other memories would fade before this one ever did.

Dad seemed to stand in the doorway for what seemed an eternity without moving, but I didn't move either, both of us taken up with the moment. We looked, we didn't speak, we didn't have to, our eyes told each other what we needed to say. It wasn't just love that was reaffirmed, but one of total understanding of how deeply we felt for each other and of course a final acknowledgement that blood didn't necessarily mean it was thicker than water. We confirmed we loved because we wanted to, there wasn't anything missing and in fact we were lucky to be two very special people that had a choice and wanted to be father and daughter. The chain that we thought should link us, and could never be, was just in our minds, we finally understood that we didn't need it.

On the way to the church Dad told me that I was the most wonderful daughter that anyone could wish for and that he was the proudest father that ever lived. He also told me if at any time I needed anything at all, or anything should happen in my life, he would always be there for me and not to worry.

Once inside the church, Dad and I took our respective positions and waited for the church bells to stop and the organist to start playing the wedding march. Dad and I looked at each other and with a gently squeeze of the hand we proceeded to walk slowly towards to the altar. Dad wasn't the most stable on his feet at the best of times and staggered, but holding onto him as tightly as I could, we managed to get there without any of the congregation noticing.

I didn't notice anyone's individual face until we reached Nigel and opposite stood my mother. She was standing next to my Auntie Ciss and Norma, and I recall she wasn't smiling, neither was she tearful like most mothers at their daughter's wedding. In fact, her expression was pretty emotionless considering the circumstances, but I shouldn't have expected anything else.

On seeing Mum's face, anger and resentment started to build up in me again. I thought how she had treated me in the past, and the hypocrisy of the poem she had just given to me, made my blood boil. I desperately wanted to ask her why she had given me the poem when we both knew we had never had that loving mother/daughter relationship which the poem so eloquently portrayed. I felt as if she had stabbed me in the back again, and I furiously wanted to shout, "Look at me, your daughter, a person you should be proud of and love unconditionally". I wanted her to understand that the only reason for marrying Nigel was to get away from her and to ask her "did the way she treat me make her feel good and give her a sadistic buzz or was it that she simply didn't care about me?"

Suddenly Dad gripped my hand a little tighter, and before I realised, I was standing next to Nigel. I remember Nigel looking at me and smiling but I can't recall smiling back, in fact, I don't believe that I did. I heard the Vicar say, "We are all gathered here today", but after that, I became oblivious to all external words other than those within my own mind.

My subconscious was bombarded with self-deprecating questions and the answers were all mixed up, some making sense, but many not. Tormented by one question after another I felt lost in a tunnel of greyness that closed in on me the deeper I went. I knew that I was gay, and I couldn't help that society wouldn't accept it. I knew I had to grasp my freedom from my mother in any way that I could, but at the same time I felt an overwhelming guilt for leaving my Dad. Irrespective of these feelings, I also felt incredibly guilty and angry with myself for allowing this day to come to fruition. How could I be so hypocritical to enter a place of worship, and ask God to bless a marriage that in all honestly was a sham. The stupid thing was, I wasn't even sure if I believed in God any more so why should I be bothered? Still standing, and blind to my surroundings, I repeatedly asked myself, what do I do? I either had to spend the rest of my life with my mother because besides marriage I couldn't ever see her letting me leave home on my own, or I had to spend the rest of my life in a marriage that I didn't want, married to a man who I didn't love. Could I be strong enough to cope with the physical side of the marriage; could I cope with the feeling every time we made love that it was not what I wanted. Suddenly the realisation of what was happening hit me and I knew I had to stop the ceremony.

Awakened from my thoughts, I became aware of my surroundings and felt a deep sense of urgency to stop myself from making a mistake. Unfortunately, it was too late, I'd somehow managed to stand through the entire ceremony, answered "I do" and even said my vows and couldn't recall a single word. Whether it was anger, too much to drink, a total mental blackout, or a combination, I soon realised that I was now a married woman instead of a single one, all be it trapped under the control of my mother.

Realisation that my life suddenly had a different meaning was hard to accept, but even more intolerable was the thought that it was Mum's fault. If only I hadn't wanted freedom from her so much, this whole situation wouldn't have happened. Unfortunately, I now had to overcome it and make the best of a bad situation. I could have cried and never stopped, but then that would have made me weak, so the remainder of the day I looked upon as a party and not a wedding reception because sooner rather than later I would come down to earth.

Although I was hurting inside, I delivered a smiling face to everyone. The day had nearly ended, the reception was good and everyone had enjoyed it. To be honest I can't remember much about it other than through the bottom of a glass of gin and tonic. That was of course, until we arrived at our hotel for the honeymoon. Nigel had booked a honeymoon suite at a hotel in Malvern. Although not a great distance to travel, it was good for a few nights and for a couple wishing to save money for a down payment on a house, which incidentally wasn't my idea. I felt trapped enough, without buying a house with him. Nigel had assumed that we would stay at Mum's for at least a few months until we found somewhere of our own. Frankly I didn't relish either prospect, but I knew that I wouldn't be buying a house with Nigel. In my mind it was obvious that the marriage wouldn't last, So, you may ask "Why get married in the first place?", and to be honest, I really cannot answer that question other than to say I saw it as a means of escape.

I figured we were better off staying at Mum's than having a fight with Nigel over where we should live, after all I was now a married woman and so she could no longer hold the same control over me. Divorce would come eventually, I was sure of that. I realised how cruel and unfair I'd been to Nigel accepting his marriage proposal, unfortunately I had to continue this lie of a marriage for the foreseeable future. Nigel didn't deserve the way I'd treated him, and yes, I could blame my mother, my mental state, but in all honesty, it was all my doing. I in turn had created a situation that would cause heartache to another individual and it was totally heartless of me. He had the right to know but how do you tell a person that you just married that in fact you are gay. He would have felt cheated and no doubt embarrassed by the whole situation, so I kept quiet.

It's a strange position to be in, standing in your hotel bathroom, knowing that your new husband is waiting in the adjacent room, and you are contemplating telling him the truth and how to get out of the marriage after only a matter of hours. The thought that he wanted to make love sickened me, and I didn't know how I was going to avoid it, and had resigned myself to the fact that I would have to lie back and take what was coming. Surprisingly, someone or something was on my side, as I realised I had started my period. With some relief, I walked into the room where Nigel was waiting sighing inwardly with relief, while explaining to Nigel my predicament. He was very understanding, although I am sure he must have felt very frustrated. Tomorrow is another day I thought, but what happens when I run out of excuses and the tomorrows are still there, what do I do then?

CHAPTER SEVEN

Quite soon after our wedding, we had started to disagree and argue about everything and nothing, but especially the emphasis was placed on the lack of sexual contact.

Inevitably the tomorrows continued to arrive, and my excuses started to wear extremely thin. On the occasions I allowed Nigel to make love to me, I felt I was being abused all over again. It made me feel cheap and dirty; I know Nigel would have been horrified if he had known because he was not a bad person and I think he really loved me.

By the third month of our marriage, a confrontation took place which was to beat all previous ones. I was surprised it had taken so long to reach that point but glad it had finally come to a head. This was the time to be honest with Nigel and tell him the truth, more so for his sake than mine. Unfortunately, when it came down to it, I still couldn't tell him. I know I was hurting him by not being a complete wife to him, but I felt torn between doing the right thing towards him and protecting myself.

It was a wonderful thought to come clean and put my farce of a marriage behind me, but I had no idea how Nigel would react to my disclosure and more importantly how it would hurt him and the effect it would have on him. There of course another concern. Nigel would no doubt inform Mum why the marriage had broken down. If that were to happen then all hells fires would have raged, the consequences of which I didn't wish to dwell on.

Nigel's pain was entirely down to me and I wished so much that I could alleviate his misery, but Mum's power and my weakness overrode any ounce of decency that I had.

For the next few months life continued much as it had before I was married. The only difference was that Nigel and I now lived where Matthew had lived. Matthew had left two months before the wedding; at least the wedding served a purpose in getting rid of him. Mum gave Matthew notice to leave, citing the reason that when Nigel and I married we would need the rooms that he had occupied for so long. Apparently Matthew returned to Ireland to live the remainder of his life with his wife. He had been given an invitation to the wedding, but I never knew for sure whether he ever accepted. I told Mum I didn't want him at the wedding, but she insisted that he should be invited. Whether he did accept or not, I don't know but I really didn't care as thankfully he did not attend.

With the sanctuary of my bedroom spoilt by Nigel's presence, I had to find another place in which to find my refuge and I found it at work. It was a place I always liked, so it became easy for me to feel happy there. I was working a forty hour week, and soon started to do overtime. It was almost like a drug that I couldn't give up, and although the money was a bonus as it allowed me to save, more importantly it gave me space and freedom from all the issues at home, and a time for me to have my thoughts uninterrupted.

When Matthew left, the two rooms he had lived in for so many years were altered to accommodate Nigel and myself. The larger room of the two was redecorated, curtains replaced and furnished with a small suit of furniture and a TV. The back room remained as a kitchen but modernised as much as the space would allow. Nigel and I spent most of our evenings here to give us privacy from Mum and Dad. This, however, wasn't really my idea of fun as I didn't enjoy being with Nigel, but in saying that I didn't wish to be in Mum's company either. It was a no-win situation and unfortunately, I had to make the most of a bad lot. The only consolation I had was the fact I knew it wouldn't last forever and patience was a virtue.

Virtue or not, this didn't stop me hating these rooms. They always appeared cold, gloomy and depressive. The contributing factors were firstly that Nigel and I had a far from warm relationship and secondly the fact that Matthew had once lived there. Somehow it didn't seem to matter that I'd changed the décor and tried to make it as comfortable as I could, it was as if Matthew's presence still existed within these walls. I constantly felt uneasy, as though Matthew was standing behind me ready to pounce and abuse me all over again. Sometimes Nigel would try to put his arms around me, and I would almost freeze to the spot in sheer panic that it was Matthew. Sometimes I would make the excuse that I wanted to sit with Dad for a while, which I knew upset Nigel, and although I liked to have some time away from Nigel, it was mainly due to the disconcerting feeling of Matthew's presence which I just could not get rid of.

On the occasions I went to sit with Dad, he was always pleased to see me. Mum I think, in her own way was too, but never made anything out of it and just carried on doing whatever it was she was doing. A few times I noticed her looking at me but her facial expression never gave anything away. They never asked why Nigel did not join me, and just accepted that I was spending time with them.

For a few weeks Dad hadn't been feeling very well and to be honest he hadn't looked too good. He had been complaining of constantly feeling tiered and a sort of shakiness which he wasn't very forthcoming about. The Doctor put it down to a chill and told him rest and in a few weeks he'd feel better. I constantly worried about Dad's health; he was my rock and the thought of anything happening to him was unbearable.

I was waiting for correspondence from the Area Health Authority as I had applied to the Ambulance Service about a vacancy for an Ambulance Driver which I'd read about in the local paper. As I had always had an interest in medical issues, and I was a member of the St Johns Ambulance, I was now considering a career with the Ambulance Service. In retrospect, I realise it wasn't just a career that I was seeking, but an occupation that would fulfil my mental needs as well as helping me to regain my own self respect and dignity. Finally, I believe it was a last endeavour to make my mother proud of the daughter I felt she had abandoned for so long. Despite how she had treated me, and no matter how much hatred I felt towards her, I still couldn't deny I wanted the opportunity to make her at least respect me. What drove me to do this I'm still not sure, but one day I hope I'll find the answer, maybe there was a spark of love for my Mum which I was still not accepting.

As luck prevailed, an interview with the Area Health Authority materialised. My education did not fulfil their requirements but, what Dad had taught me during the previous two years certainly helped. I was told at the time that my lack of education gave them cause for concern and under normal circumstances would have been a most definite failure, but due to my honesty, enthusiasm, advanced driving certificate which I had passed only a few weeks prior, my first aid knowledge plus my shear guts and determination they would offer me employment.

Suddenly, I'd done it, I had achieved a modicum of success; I was on the pay roll of an organisation that was run by the Government and the Queen for that matter, not that I was a royalist by any stretch of the imagination, but now I'd achieved an important and real meaning to my life. For once I felt good about myself and it was wonderful. I remembered thinking, surely Mum would have to acknowledge and respect me, after all I was now in professional employment.

These two important factors to me were, however, to lead to disappointment. Mum congratulated me in a half-hearted manner, showing she did not value or appreciate the significance to me of gaining this milestone in my life, and because of that I assumed her respect for me hadn't grown either. Oh well, I tried.

As for the job, my enthusiasm hit rock bottom within the space of only a few weeks. Ignorantly I thought Ambulance Service only dealt with accidents and emergencies, but unfortunately I found out otherwise very quickly. In fact, at that particular time the

Ambulance Service worked on the principal of a two tier system, and I was employed on the lower tier, which involved transporting patients to and from hospital. My first aid knowledge was not used and so did not improve, and I became unsettled and despondent, and I suppose a little disappointed. Every day I would watch the Ambulance Men answer an emergency call, see their enthusiasm and feel the adrenaline they must have felt rush through their body. I wanted so much to be part of that lifesaving team, but I wasn't. Yes, I was in the Ambulance Service, I had a uniform and some responsibilities, but it didn't stimulate me enough. I didn't want people to be hurt, but I so wanted to be part of the team that was in a position to treat and ease the anguish of people who found themselves in a desperate situation. I craved the knowledge and skills others had and to be able to achieve the same results, and as much as I'm ashamed to admit it, I was not put off by the blood, vomit and guts that came with it. The added thrill and excitement from the burst of adrenaline also appealed to me, and strangely enough, having always wanted to be the person in the background, I now wanted to be noticed by people and be in a position to take control of the situation.

Like many people who get their confidence by dressing in a certain way or behaving non- conservatively, my uniform gave me the confidence that I needed. I knew if I could achieve qualifications in the Ambulance Service it would enhance my self-esteem and allow me to break away from the feeling of total failure I had carried with me for most of my life.

On the two separate occasions I applied to be considered for further training, my applications were refused on the grounds that women were not employed on emergency crews. This I found unbelievable, as the neighbouring Metropolitan Service did. As I was considering transferring to this Authority, which I really didn't want to do because of the travelling expenses, the law changed as regards equal opportunities for women. Thankfully this gave me another chance to re-apply but before I did, I had to confirm that my station officer would be prepared to give me his backing. Not only did he do this, but he also showed me some lifting techniques and agreed I was as strong as any of the men and in some cases even stronger!

My application was accepted, and I successfully passed the lifting test, and was told further training would be considered. All the men on the station congratulated me and said I'd pass with ease. An interview with the Chief and the Entrance Test had been arranged for the following week, in the meantime the men including the Station Officer rallied around to ensure my lifting techniques were correct.

My Station Officer was a good man, who always had every confidence in my ability and that meant everything to me. The day of the test arrived which in all honesty, to this day, I'm convinced was a set up to keep me quiet. I have never believed for one minute that the test was to assess my competence in lifting, but just a ploy on behalf of the Chief to finally stop my endeavours to progress.

To be frank, the Chief was a man I never liked or trusted but then half the employees didn't like him either. Unfortunately, he was a man who looked upon himself as a man's man and his domain was a man's world. Women could fulfil the mundane administrative work that existed, but were not welcome within the higher realms of the service. I believe he had the attitude of running a men's only club.

The test itself, although I had no proof, was his endeavour to prevent me or any woman from applying in the future. Although sex equality was now law, there were ways around it, and it hadn't been tested to any great extent. Under normal circumstances the lifting would have been carried out with a qualified competent male member of staff, but in my case it wasn't. I underwent the examination with another woman that had the strength of a gnat.

The Chief asked to see me afterwards and with an apologetic grin, he informed me that I had failed. I pointed out that I wasn't very happy with his decision and asked why I hadn't had the regular test with a male member of staff, and requested a fair re-test, but he refused, also refusing to answer any of my questions. He did however point out that the new equality law wasn't a bad thing but in some vocations, it was better left to the men to handle.

That was it, his decision was final. Even though I knew he was wrong what could I do to fight him and if I had my life would have been hell. Leaving Headquarters and making my way back to the station I realised I hadn't got a future within the Authority, and if I wished to pursue this job as a career, I had no other choice than to transfer to another authority. If that was my only option, I knew during my twelve month training period I would have to survive with very little money, but I had savings so I would be able to manage.

As I pulled onto the station car park, I saw Peter, my Station Officer through his office window, and he mouthed "how did you get on?" As soon as I had parked the Ambulance, I walked across the garage, went into his office and closed the door behind me. I burst into tears from the sheer disappointment I felt, shedding tears I had held back for so many years. Eventually, forcing myself to calm down, I told Peter about the whole farce and what I truly suspected. He told me not to worry, go and have a cup of tea and he would try his best to find out what had happened and hopefully persuade the Chief that I should be retested as he knew there was nothing wrong with my strength.

I made myself a drink and each time I brough the cup to my lips I'd start crying again. I so desperately wanted to be a Qualified Ambulance woman. The knowledge of knowing that I shouldn't have failed, was tearing me apart and once again I felt cheated and intimidated by men in a position of perceived power.

Sometime later, still sitting with a half drunken cup of tea, Peter walked in and sat down beside me. I knew by his expression and how he acted he hadn't managed to achieve anything. "Right then" he said putting his arm around me and I immediately started crying again, he continued "it's all fixed. I've had a word and you've passed your lifting test, and you should be on your Ambulance Aid course in approximately three months' time. Are you happy now"? I just sat there. I heard what he said but was waiting for it to register. Within a few minutes it had registered, and I started crying all over again, but this time through relief.

I never knew until some years later, when the Chief had retired, what really happened the day Peter phoned him. Apparently, Peter had questioned the failure and pointed out that he knew differently and that I was thinking of taking the matter to the Area Health Authority. By all accounts he overturned his decision within seconds.

Despite my mistrust of men in general, I always found Peter to be a very honest person who stood by his principles and fairness, but above all, without him I wouldn't have been given a chance and for that very reason I was forever in his debt with special thanks and respect.

Because of my obvious distress and then relief, Peter felt I would be better at home and gave me the rest of the day off. I didn't have a clue why I was continuing to cry, but now I understand all too well that the experience of being told that I had failed was the final straw that had destroyed my hopes and ambitions for the future. Me, the hard person that wouldn't allow anyone or anything to hurt me, had crumbled.

When I got home, Dad calmed me down and when I told him I felt silly for crying he told me not to worry it was just a conflict of emotions that had got on top of me. That was true enough, but subconsciously I knew it wasn't the whole reason.

Surprisingly when Mum returned home from work that evening, to my surprise and amazement she acted completely differently to how I'd become accustomed. She was kind and thoughtful. She looked like my mother in every respect, but her attitude had changed so drastically I thought perhaps she'd been taken over by an alien force or had a brain and heart transplant without me knowing. She was hugging me while I started crying all over again and gave me the support and comfort I so desperately needed. In fact, for once in my life she was being a mother, which made my tears flow even stronger and quicker, and for a brief moment I saw a tear coming from her as well.

I couldn't believe I was still upset over something that had turned out alright in the end, but obviously I didn't realise the true significance and have had to wait until now to understand the true effect it had on me.

Although a solitary tear followed the contours of Mum's face, all I wanted to do was pull away. I didn't feel able to deal with her emotion and the affection she was now showing me. For a moment it felt natural and wonderful to be comported by my Mum, but sadly the feeling changed to anger, vulnerability and panic about these strange and unfamiliar emotions I was experiencing. I had longed for so long to have the closeness with her that I thought should be natural for mother and daughter, but it was just too much to cope with in the emotional state I found myself in.

Although my instincts told me that her affection wasn't false, I found I couldn't reciprocate the affection, as strangely enough it had already increased by sense of insecurity. Still crying, I realised the tears were now for the confusion I felt toward Mums' unexpected openness and warmth. The hug she had given me had certainly felt good, but there was no denying it hurt, not physically, but mentally it confused me. An act that was so out of character and unexpected touched a part of my soul that I thought I'd locked away forever. The sad thing was, the love and affection I'd longed for had finally come, but as much as I wanted to accept it, my memories reminded me that inevitably I would end up getting hurt when the affection was withdrawn for some minor misdemeanour.

Three months later, I was finally on my way to start my residential Ambulance training course. The course itself lasted for six weeks and after successfully completing this, there was another twelve months training on the road in your own authority.

I can never recall being as nervous as I was on that first day. Excited, but also feeling a considerable amount of pressure to do well. First and foremost, this was for my own benefit, but it was also for my Station Officer who believed and stood by me.

The first two weeks of the course, I must be honest, I didn't know whether I was coming or going and questioned many times if I'd done the right thing. The hours spent in the classroom being bombarded about various systems of the body confused me. From nucleus to mitochondria of a living cell; from sympathetic and para-sympathetic nervous systems; they all had my mind boggled. My Bible, the anatomy and physiology books were never far away from reach, as too was my dictionary to aid my spelling. My education, or lack of, hampered my learning ability, at times making it twice as hard to learn.

We had to learn about the human structure and every function of the body, with signs and symptoms of multiple conditions, injuries and their treatments. Infectious diseases, basic and tropical; from drugs to gases; mental health and associated law; childbirth, natural and complicated; equipment and rescue techniques.

The course was a mixed-up jumble of data that I believed would never make sense. I, like all the others on the course, was constantly being brain washed with so many facts and figures I wondered if I'd ever be the same again. In fact, at the end of the course, I wasn't the same person at all and through my hard work not only did my confidence improve, so did my reading, writing, and spelling, but in addition I passed the course.

On the last day, the exam results were given by a simple pass or fail which was done to stop any embarrassment, but a private informal chat afterwards with the head instructor was also on the agenda. Although I already knew I had passed, I had wondered by what percentage and as the minimum was seventy-two percent, I anticipated I probably just scraped through. The chat with the instructor however revealed otherwise to my astonishment and in fact out of forty trainees, I came second with a remarkable ninety-seven percent. In truth, this information took some considerable time to digest, and I just sat amazed while he continued talking. It wasn't until I heard him say he was going to recommend to my authority that I should be put forward to obtain the Fellowship of Ambulance Service Personnel that I came back to my senses. After questioning his remark, he continued to tell me that he had no doubts that I could achieve it and I'd be a fool not to go for it. It was a nice thought that in a years' time, when I'd completed the training out on the road, I could explore that possibility. Only a handful of officers in my authority held it, and I knew it was extremely difficult but I wasn't in any rush and for once in my life, with my sheer strength and determination, I had achieved what I thought was the impossible, I'd regained by dignity, self-respect and above all my happiness. It was good to think I could progress in the future to obtain the F.A.S.P because for the first time since I could remember, I felt good about myself.

Having passed my exam, I was now expected to turn my theoretical knowledge into practice on real patients, and members of the public. This I admit felt a daunting prospect, but as a senior qualified member of staff would be assigned to me on every emergency call for the following twelve months, I knew I would learn more from him about the real complexity and practicality of the job than I had done on the course – there is nothing like firsthand experience.

Although in theory I'd learnt and seen a great deal at training school in lectures, films, pictures, make up and role play, it didn't prepare me for the human destruction of life and loss of dignity people suffered in times of distress. It wasn't just the patients to think about, but often their families suffered extreme emotional state of shock on these occasions and I hadn't accounted for that.

Generally, the attendant was always the one in charge and this was done on alternative day about pattern, but as I was still training, patient care was ultimately the Senior Crew Member's responsibility and at any time he felt I hadn't the relevant experience, then he would take over. This was fine until unfortunately a situation arose whereby we were faced with more than one seriously injured casualty.

An incident occurred on one of my first emergency calls. I had always been told that I'd be either gently eased into the job or the opposite, and I'd be thrown in at the deep end. Well to be honest, it certainly wasn't the shallow end, that was for sure.

After returning from my course, I was given a new contract of employment stating I was now a relief

Ambulance Woman. This meant covering for sickness or leave in the whole of the Authority, but as the authority was Hereford and Worcestershire the mileage at times covered some considerable distance. Although, now employed as a relief I didn't start to carry out these duties until some two months later, when I worked with a man called Richard from my station. He had already got a regular colleague but within six months his colleague left, and I became Richard's regular partner and remained so for many years.

I recall one Saturday when Richard's mate had gone sick and I was called in to do his eight-hour shift. It must have been around ten thirty and suddenly all hell let loose, and I was placed in the position of make or break.

Just fifteen minutes into the shift and we were pulling up behind a twisted carnage of metal that involved three vehicles. The accident had happened at the crossroads called five ways which was situated in a semi-rural location that was always an accident black spot.

As Richard brought the ambulance to a halt, he told me, as it looked a bad accident I could be on my own as there would be too many casualties to stick together. He told me not to worry, don't rush and I'd be just fine. Remember your priorities he continued and also remember the people least hurt are normally the ones that do most shouting. Concentrate on the quieter ones first. At this Richard left the ambulance without waiting for a reply and I was left to exit the vehicle myself, but nervously misplaced my footing and tumbled down the steps onto the road. I quickly righted myself, filling my lungs with fresh air and proceeded to walk towards the entangled pile of metal that stood before me.

In the mass of destruction and chaos, I spotted a baby of no more than eighteen months lying in the middle of the road. He was lying on his back with his right arm stretched above his head and the other underneath his twisted small innocent body. His eyes which once moved, remained wide fixed and staring into space. This little child without so much as a mark on his body lay lifeless and cold. His stillness was a harsh reality that he no longer remained a part of this world.

Standing to the side, a four- or five-year-old child was crying uncontrollably and looking hopelessly lost. A trickle of blood on her forehead had started to dry.

My instinct was to hold and cradle both children and although I knew the one was dead, it somehow didn't matter. I just wanted to comfort them both.

I almost lost my reason for being there; a tug of war between my training and my maternal instinct raged within me, as I was torn between my knowledge, skills and professionalism, and the emotional and physical support I yearned to give to a child in need. It was an experience that training school hadn't prepared me for, let alone described how to deal with. In fact, the answer is you have to be strong enough to cut yourself off from these emotions and deal with the situation in a professional way. This probably sounds hard, but this was something I learnt to do very quickly, otherwise I realised the emotional drain placed on me would become overpowering and destructive, preventing me doing my job.

POST SCRIPT

As one of the first women to serve in Hereford &
Worcester Ambulance Service on emergencies, Shane
experienced discrimination; male colleagues refusing to
work with her on nights; being told she was not strong
enough to do the job. However, in the end she was
recognised as a very competent Ambulance Person and
well respected by her work team mates. Unfortunately,
her career was brought to an abrupt end when she had
a fall at work and injured her back. The injury was
so severe it resulted in her being unable to do her job,
and so she was pensioned off. There was very little
in the way of rehabilitation or offers of alternative
employment, so Shane found herself in the unenviable
position of no longer being able to do the job she loved.

Unsurprisingly, Shane and Nigel divorced and Shane
went on to have gay relationships, finally accepting her
sexuality. She continued to struggle with trust and
found it difficult to give full commitment because of her
wariness of getting too close to anyone. Perhaps this
was partly to blame for the breakdown of her
relationships.

One particular split left Shane broken as it was her
partner and a close friend who cheated on her, having
an affair. Her only solace was the company of her
beloved Margo who was her Boxer dog. Shane was left
in a difficult financial position, so when a good friend

offered to lend her the money to have Margo covered, she took the offer knowing she would earn some desperately needed cash from selling the puppies, although her priority would always be to ensure they went to good homes. It would also give her something to concentrate on over the next few months as she tried to heal the wounds of yet another betrayal.

We pick Shane's narration up as she starts looking for a new relationship having been on her own for some time.

PART TWO

RUNNING SCARED

CHAPTER ONE

I first met Grace on a Friday night 4th June 1994, not that I'm usually any good at remembering dates. We had previously spoken on the telephone, and it appeared our tastes and general outlook on life were very similar, if not uncannily a mirror image.

We had agreed to meet at The Stag public house, which was an Inn at a place called Red Hill in the district of Stratford Upon Avon. Although I had met several women in the previous weeks with the view to making new friendships, none had come to anything, but I was intrigued to meet this woman. I felt a state of nervousness that I hadn't sensed with any of the others and found it difficult to rid myself of this feeling.

The conversation with Grace only two nights before, had been extremely easy and needed very little effort at all. In fact, it was worrying how easy it was, especially when I find the art of conversation difficult, bordering on impossible at the best of times.

Deep down I was panicking because most of the subjects had already been covered on the telephone. Suddenly the thought of being face to face with someone I appeared to have so much in common with, frightened me and I started questioning my wisdom agreeing to meet her. Would I dry up or get stage struck and look a complete fool or worst still a total moron.

I realise a lot of people would find it hard to comprehend that someone at the age of thirty-nine, would find it difficult and even panic at the sheer thought of having a conversation with someone. Most people are unaware of the gift of conversation, and do not appreciate just how lucky they are. In fact, their communication skills alone easily provide them with the opportunity to make friends, admitted not all are genuine and some can be loosely termed as friends, but never the less, there natural ability to converse allows friendships to develop, whereas for me, it never did.

Without wanting to contradict myself, I did have two very good friends. Lyn who I'd had a relationship with some years ago and Victoria who lived not very far from me in the same road. Both were friends who would always be there for me in my hour of need and I for them. However, I needed a relationship with someone who shared my own interests and ambitions to achieve certain goals in life.

Grace seemed to share so many of the same ideals as I did, but I was scared witless of blowing it. After just one telephone call I hoped that we could become friends as it was obvious we had the same interests. Having lived most of my life without many friends, including my childhood years due to my own fear and self-protection, I now recognised my need to rectify this and the need of friendship. Unsurprisingly my marriage to Nigel ended in divorce and subsequently, being true to myself, I had a number of relationships with women. Sadly, none worked out and I had been let down and cheated on, so my confidence was at an all-time low. Although it was exciting to think I may be embarking on a new episode in my life, it was also frightening beyond explanation.

My friendships with Lyn and Victoria had evolved over time. With Lyn it was a case of two lonely mixed-up gay women jumping into a relationship. For me it was to escape the memory of nursing and then the bereavement of my parents, and for Lyn, it allowed her to escape a marriage and its implications which weren't natural to her. It wasn't until some years after our relationship came to an end, we became friends and never looked back.

My friendship with Victoria came from my relationship with Kelly. She was in fact Kelly's friend, and although I was always included, I still used to find it difficult to converse with people who were unfamiliar to me. This continued for the seven years that Kelly and I were together. Unfortunately, when Kelly and I separated she cut all ties with Victoria as well. Because Victoria lived just a few doors away, I continued to see her and from then on, our friendship became stronger.

I had reached a time in my life when I understood how important friendships were, and I realised I couldn't continue to live the lonely solitary life I thought I wanted. The only problem was I didn't want to be second best again and I wasn't going to jump into bed again either. I wanted someone to like me for who I was and hoped that Grace wouldn't think I was an idiot for wanting to take things slowly.

The journey to The Stag took approximately twenty minutes and on arrival I parked in one of the car parking spaces at the furthest end of the car park, away from the main entrance to the pub. At least from there I could see cars coming and going along the entrance drive from the main road. I checked my watch for the time, which showed twenty-five past seven, I always preferred to be early than late for any appointment. Part of me wanted to restart the car and get the hell out of there. My nerves had started to get the better of me, but unfortunately before I had a chance, I noticed a white Skoda driving past and heading for the car park. Within seconds it parked beside me, and I watched as the occupant, Grace I assumed, got out of the car. She had an open, smiling face and I immediately felt some of my nerves evaporating as she looked my way and smiled. There was no going back now, so I got out of the car and introduced myself. We walked together to the entrance, chatting about our respective journey.

Once inside the pub, which is a seventeenth century coach house that I'd passed on many occasions but never visited before, my nervousness, surprisingly, started to further abate. The evening was very pleasurable and sitting in a corner seat beside an open fire, I found myself relaxing in Grace's company and at ease for the first time in years.

As it had been on the telephone, the conversation was easy and neither of us paused for breath. In fact, we were so engrossed, the landlord asked us to leave as the bar had closed and we were the only people remaining.

We arranged to meet again at The Stag on Sunday lunchtime and spend the rest of the day together. As Grace didn't know the area very well, it seemed an ideal place to meet, and she could follow me home.

Lunch went well, and as agreed Grace followed me back to Redditch. Once at home, she immediately fell in love with my dog Margo. To this day I'm still not sure whether it was in fact Margo that she fell in love with, or me! but whichever, there was an immediate bonding between the two of them.

Margo was my Boxer and I loved her unconditionally. We had been through a lot together over the past few months, and I was so glad to see her happy and have an aura of love surround her once more. It was as if meeting Grace gave her a new lease of life. She seemed to instantly change her mood and character; she was no longer sad and depressed, which she had been for some time, or was this me?

It wasn't Margo's fault she felt so insecure, upset and miserable. If Margo had felt anything like I had for the last few months, she too had been living on her nerves and was probably as distressed as I was but at least now, it seemed that Margo had put it behind her. It was heart-warming to see a friendship between Margo and Grace, as for Grace and myself, well that remained to be seen, but it felt good even if it did feel alien to me.

I had recently gone through a very traumatic break up of a seven-year relationship. What had made it worse, was someone I thought was a friend and I could trust had an affair with my Partner. Between the two of them they managed to destroy any trust I had started to build up over the years. My life had changed dramatically when I had an accident at work resulting in a back injury which prevented me from working, and I was pensioned off by the Ambulance Service. It had taken me some years to come to terms with the fact I could not work but when I eventually met Kelly, I thought I could see a life together. She seemed to understand and accept my situation and we settled into a comfortable routine. We both had a love for the Caribbean and were able to holiday in Jamaica on several occasions. When we decided to add a companion to our family, we chose Margo. Margo was our sole mate, she went everywhere with us and shared in our happy as well as the sad times. She always knew if one of us was down and would come and cuddle up giving that wet boxer kiss. But when Kelly had the affair, and the relationship was irrevocably breaking down, Margo was caught in the middle. We had some horrendous arguments during which Margo would cower in the kitchen, not knowing which one of us she should go to for comfort. As Kelly spent more and more time away from home, I slipped into a deep depression and was unable to function, totally incapable of looking after myself, let alone Margo. I didn't know which day of the week it was or how I was going to get through it, and so I took the easy option by going down to Sussex to try and get away from it all. Obviously, I couldn't stay there for long, and had to return just two week later, but it had given Kelly time to decide our relationship was over and she would be moving out. It was agreed that Margo would stay with me, and for that I will always be truly grateful. I am not sure how I would have managed without her. She was my confident, my comfort and my companion during some very dark times.

Suddenly going from a household with two incomes, to just one put a huge pressure on my finances. We had accumulated some debts, which I still had to meet as well as the day-to-day expenses of running a house. Margo had already had one litter of puppies, and she had been a brilliant mother and I had been able to find the most wonderful people to have the puppies. I had vetted them all and was sure they were suitable parents. If I could have another litter, the sale of the puppies would go some way to clearing my debts. The last thing I wanted to do was to use Margo as a "cash cow", but I felt sure she would want to help and play her part in our predicament. A very good friend lent me the money to allow me to have her mated. Although she easily became pregnant, the upsets of the previous months were having their effect, and she was not the happy mother to be she had been the first-time round – that was until Grace came into our lives.

Grace and I spent the day together as we had planned by walking the dog through the woods opposite the house. We talked, threw sticks for Margo to fetch, sat on a bench and then walked some more, realising we had more in common than first thought. After our walk, the remainder of the afternoon went just as pleasantly, in the garden enjoying a drink and the warm June sunshine.

We were engrossed in each other, laughing when funny or a nod of understanding when serious. Whatever the topic, the time flew by as quickly as the birds did in the turquoise blue sky.

In such a short time I couldn't believe how comfortable I felt in Grace's company. I can only describe it as a gift from God, as I had never felt like this with anyone before. At one stage, and I almost feel silly for saying this, but it was like I had stepped out of body and was watching myself conversing and enjoying the company of a stranger. It was like I was watching myself as though I was stranger, someone I did not recognise. I could see it was me and yet I wasn't acting anything like me. I wondered where that sad and extremely shy person had gone. The transformation was something verging on disbelief, and I wanted to continue the excitement of following this unknown path of adventure that lay ahead.

An adventure certainly lay ahead; an adventure that even with the sixth sense I had learnt to develop, I couldn't have predicted. I was starting a journey of discovery and to experience the true meaning of life to its fullest extent. A road that was by no means straight but had many twists and turns and with every bend, another piece of the jigsaw of my life would slot into place.

A journey had started with Grace, and we had so much in common, I felt sure our friendship could develop into something meaningful and long lasting. Although I had promised I would not succumb to anything physical on this first meeting, a single kiss ended up with us making love. After, I was so disappointed with myself and felt it was less a matter of making love, but rather a release of emotions, which wasn't fair on either of us. I felt I'd had to depend on a sexual side to our meeting, rather than relying on a genuine closeness developing from our friendship. I was certainly attracted to Grace, and I know the feelings were mutual, but this did not stop me from feeling I had let myself down.

In a mad stupid moment of desire, I felt a unique friendship had been lost forever, tainted and it would never be the same again. I hadn't given us a chance to form a bond without sex influencing our relationship and I was sure I had blown any chance of this now developing into anything truly meaningful.

Grace soon left on her long journey home. I could see the experience had disturbed her and the sense of regret saddened her as it did me. I wondered if she would ever contact me again or whether we would go our separate ways, and put it down to a casual sexual encounter.

I wasn't sure what had happened other than I knew a lovely day had been spoilt and I couldn't see how it could ever be the same again. Fortunately, that evening Grace telephoned to say that she'd arrived home safely and thanked me for a lovely time. The conversation eventually turned to the subject of the physical contact, and we agreed it wasn't what either of us wanted. It was left that Grace would phone me over the forthcoming weeks. That was it as far as I was concerned, the friendship was over before it had begun. I prepared myself for never receiving another telephone call from Grace because I thought she wouldn't bother. However, Wednesday came and much to my surprise Grace phoned to ask if she could call in and see me, plus she had managed to get some bricks for me as she knew I was in the process of building a wall.

We had several meetings in the following fortnight, each one ending as we had already agreed it wouldn't, with physical contact in varying degrees. Somehow the more we said friendship was the only thing we wanted the more physical and emotional we became.

Because of the distance apart that we lived, we only saw each other on a weekend and during the week we would telephone one another. This arrangement, at the time, was ideal as we could still have our own space and independence.

Margo had given birth to ten lovely puppies, and when we decided Grace would spend her two-week summer holiday with us, she was a huge help with the puppies, giving me a complete rest which was a welcome break as it is hard work looking after ten puppies.

By the end of the holiday all of the puppies had been sold and had gone to their new homes, except for one bitch that we were going to call Charlie. We had already decided she would be going nowhere. Grace had fallen in love with her and she seemed like a good companion for Margo. The Friday before Grace was due to return to work on the Monday, we were both feeling sad and down in the dumps at the thought of her departure on Sunday. We had already discussed the possibilities of Grace moving to Redditch and living together, but this couldn't be done overnight, which meant we would have to live separate lives in the week.

Sunday came and we hardly spoke to each other, both upset that in a few hours we would be apart, so we remained quiet and in our own thoughts. Fortunately, Grace came up with a suggestion which could solve the dilemma. Why couldn't I go to her house and stay in the week, and we would come back to Birchfield Road for the weekend. After some thought it was agreed that all four of us would go to Banbury.

Within an hour we were packed, including the dogs and on our way. It was as if a big black cloud had suddenly disappeared and the sadness had gone as we looked forward to a new stage in our relationship.

Some months had passed since our first meeting and our friendship had grown a hundred-fold, as had our relationship. Strangely, although neither of us had wanted a physical relationship, the times we weren't close felt unnatural. At this stage I am not sure I can say it was love, but more likely lust which drove our physical relationship. But as time passed, I sensed a feeling of belonging to each other, and I could see our friendship was becoming stronger, bound together as one, without us even realising.

I cannot say what was most important to Grace, but for me, the friendship came first. I had started to build trust in Grace, although every instinct told me to fight this as I had been betrayed and let down so many times in the past. Perhaps I was tired of fighting my battles, and I was letting my guard down, but I was finding it increasingly difficult to fight the trust I was placing in Grace and hoped it would not prove to be misplaced.

For the following four months we lived in Banbury during the week and returned to Redditch for the weekend. I had always thought Redditch had become extremely overpopulated with very little countryside but staying at Grace's made me realise where I was in Redditch was almost in the country. There were many times that we would pass the comment that on a weekend we were going to or country retreat. But the commuting between the two places was not ideal, and so Grace put her mind to finding new job in Redditch which would mean we could live permanently at Birchfield Road.

By Christmas she had found a job in Redditch which started in the New Year and by Christmas eve Grace and her belongings had moved in; now we were officially a couple, living together full time.

It was a funny sort of Christmas as Grace had only moved in the day before Christmas, and we hadn't had time to unwind and relax, let alone get each other a Christmas present or even to say Happy Christmas and savour our first Christmas together. Christmas hadn't been the same since Mum and Dad had passed away, but as I had already met Grace's Mum and Dad on a few occasions, I was invited to spend Christmas day and Boxing Day with them, but would travel home at night to see the dogs. I felt slight trepidation at the thought of spending Christmas with people I didn't know, however they made me very welcome, and I tried to fit in the best I could, even if did feel somewhat out of place and out of my depth.

With Christmas over and New Year's Eve arrived, Grace and I had been invited to a party by a friend who lived in Bromsgrove, about six miles away. This was the first gay party we had been to, and so the first time we could dance and kiss without feeling embarrassed. With the first strike of Big Ben at midnight we wished everyone a Happy New Year. Grace and I kept our wishes to the last and that was when I felt my trust in mankind had returned, and that was thanks to Grace. The depth of love I felt for her astounded me. I knew that I had fallen in love with her, but until now I had not realised how deep those feelings went. We had exchanged rings in the previous August, and I knew then that I loved her, but during the past months that love had deepened, and I recognised this was a totally different emotion to any I had previously experienced. It was 1995 and we were about to start to live life to the full, I felt there was a bright future ahead of us.

Grace started her new job on January 4th 1995. It took a few weeks to adjust to working permanent days as she was used to working a rotating early and late shift pattern in Banbury. With Grace's experience there was never any worries of her finding a job in Redditch, the only difference between jobs in Banbury and Redditch was the salary. In Banbury Grace received a far higher salary than she could earn in Redditch.

However, before long she had settled down and in a matter of three months, she was asked to apply for promotion to team leader in another department in the factory, which would have increased her salary. She did eventually fill in the application form and was subsequently interviewed and asked if the position were offered to her, would she accept it. Grace did not refuse outright but explained that she had heard the team leader in her department was going to be made up to supervisor, and she would prefer to take over her old job as team leader than move to another section of the factory. The only problem was, the Personnel Officer could not guarantee that the team leader position would become available and suggested it would be beneficial for Grace to take the position in the other department if it was offered to her. I did my best to persuade her to accept the position as I could clearly read between the lines, but she was adamant she wasn't going to another department. The inevitable happened, the team leader in her department wasn't made up and Grace wasn't offered another position. This brought about an unsettled and disappointed reaction in Grace, which I had not seen before, and she became disgruntled and started looking for another job.

It was now ten months since our first meeting, and a lot had certainly happened in what was a short period of time. However, some emotional instability had started to affect me mentally. I had without consciously realising become totally involved with Grace and put my trust in her. Over the previous months Grace had managed, where others had not, to encourage me to question myself about various hard and unspoken memories. On many occasions I tried to change the subject as it was too painful to recount. This was always over taken by Grace's eagerness to help me address my demons by encouraging me to talk and discuss the issues, part of me always suspected it was curiosity rather than her compassion to help me. I became confused, questioning why I wanted to reveal my innermost secrets, but I found I couldn't stop. It was as if I had to continue even if it meant self-destruction and that's exactly what I felt was happening. I wondered if Grace knew this and was aware of the possible consequences, but still she continued to pick at the bones like a bird of prey. Was I beginning to regret the trust I had placed in her?

I know I had started to despise her for what she was doing to me. If she loved me like I loved her then I could not understand why she was putting me through this self-analysis. I remember her telling me on many occasions if I talked about the past then I would rid myself of all the anger and hurt I felt, and subsequently this would make me a happier and more compassionate person. I suppose it was these remarks and her willingness to understand me, together with her caring and loving attitude, that made me continue.

By the middle of May 1995, I was struggling to deal with the emotions from this continual reflection over my past. I was finding it increasingly difficult to concentrate on the normal daily activities. Day and night my mind was in a constant turmoil reliving past memories, which I had locked away for so many years, and now seemed very real again. Reliving them felt worse than at the time. Examining every episode of my life was painful, and the hurt so much more intense than I had originally suffered. I tried to reason with myself and kept thinking of what Grace said, that I would come out a far better person; but to be frank, I'd started to think Grace knew nothing of what this was doing to me and I seriously began to resent her for making me talk about and relive my past. I now realise that anyone embarking on a journey of revisiting their past in an attempt to understand and find some peace of mind, should do this with a professional who can give the guidance and support needed to deal with the emotions experienced.

Grace had become a very prominent figure in my life. She had that get up and go and before I could blink a job had been done and she was on to the next. She was loving, thoughtful and cared for me and as I suffered with severe back problems following the accident at work, she took on the responsibility of the garden and other tasks I found it almost impossible to do since my accident.

In return I looked after the house doing most of the housework, cooking and general housekeeping. I loved her a great deal, but questioned whether she should be acting as a councillor, something she had no experience in. She did not recognise that making me talk about my past was wrong and causing me pain in a way I had never suffered before. On many occasions I wanted to stop and tried to change the subject, but Grace always managed to persuade me to start talking again. I could argue that if I hadn't wanted to talk, then I wouldn't have but it wasn't as easy as that. She had a way about her that convinced you that she was right and whatever happened she would always be there to protect me. She had the ability to make me feel dependent on her by lowering my guard, and obviously at the time I felt safe and secure.

Eventually all the talking had finished, and I had told my story, so according to Grace I should have closure on my past and be the better person I so wanted. Unfortunately trying to achieve closure and achieving it are very different. I felt I still needed to talk about some aspects of my past before I could have closure, but Grace had now got bored and started complaining this was now taking over our lives, and I needed to move on. She had no idea of the hornets' nest she had stirred by starting me down this route of self-analysis. I realised I had been fooling myself for many years that the events I thought had been successfully placed to the back of my mind, were in fact just beneath the surface.

Grace had manged to find herself a new job working for a local bailiff. She couldn't have been happier as she wished to get back into an office environment. The excitement of this new position unfortunately lasted a mere three weeks before she walked out. There were two fundamental expertise needed for this job and until she started hadn't realised what they were. As the position meant dealing with people and recovering their debts, either in cash or goods to the value of the debt, firstly Grace needed to be sufficiently objective to instruct the bailiffs to attend the property despite the circumstances, which at times she found very difficult, and secondly she needed good computer skills, which for Grace were non-existent other than being able to write a letter.

Grace's supervisor was a hard-faced woman who showed no compassion for clients and staff alike. She provided no support or training for Grace and bearing in mind that Grace's computer skills were extremely limited, the actions of the supervisor left me with the opinion that she enjoyed playing sadistic power games with her staff. She convinced Grace that she was a complete waste of space on a computer, and instead of helping her, she left her trying to work it out for herself. The final show down came after the supervisor hit Grace across the hand; the next day Grace handed in her notice. This experience had serious consequences on Grace's self-confidence. This was a great shame as she had good qualities to offer an employer, and with some training I am sure her computer skills would have improved, but unfortunately one bad person can have a seriously detrimental effect on even the strongest minded. I tried to support her in the best way I could, but I found it very difficult as I was going through my own crisis.

It was about three months before she found another job, which brough us into the middle of August 1995. Grace hadn't worried about money, as she had rented her house out in March, and therefore with money to pay the bills and a little extra, finding a job was not a priority. Unfortunately, her overdraught had virtually reached the maximum, and so there was now some urgency for her to find a new position.

She had changed since her run in at the Bailiffs; she wasn't the same outgoing individual I knew. It was as if all the stuffing had been taken away from her, and what didn't help was the fact she had started drinking more than normal.

In my mixed-up world, I was sad to see her like this especially as just six months ago she had been full of life and arranged a surprise fortieth birthday for me.

She had planned a weekend away in London. We were booked into The Plaza on Hyde Park and on Saturday went to the theatre to see Miss Saigon for the matinee performance. This was finished off with a delightful meal at a Chinese Restaurant in the evening. The Sunday we walked arm in arm through Hyde Park. It was a lovely weekend and I felt grateful, very much in love and to be perfectly honest, I didn't want it to end, but of course it always does. At the time, we didn't seem to have a care in the world, how quickly things can change in just a matter of a months.

We had decided to make a commitment to each other in August 1994. In fact, it was when Grace was staying with me during her August holiday. Many people would say we made this commitment to each other far too quickly and it wasn't love at all but infatuation. That was something only time would tell, but although I thought I had loved before, I had never felt I was in love before. I hoped with Grace this was the real thing which would last forever.

In those days there were no Civil Partnerships and not many Churches would offer Blessings, so our commitment took place on the twelfth of August at the local church, sitting outside on a bench. It was quarter to three in the afternoon, we wore jeans and tee shirts, because to us it wasn't about what we looked like, but what we said and felt. It was more a conversation with just the two of us there, and even though we tried to be serious we found ourselves laughing. It was a joyous occasion and we took our commitment very seriously, making our promises to each other, we asked God to protect us individually and as a couple; instead of offering each other wine, we drank a small amount of Holy Water that I had brought back from Lordes on a visit I'd made some years before.

In the evening, we had a table booked at a Thai Restaurant in Stratford. I felt like a queen that night. Grace had arranged everything and all I had to do was sit back and enjoy it. After the exchange of rings at the Church Grace had presented me with a lovely bouquet of twelve red roses which were out of this world and of course made me cry. This was very rare for me as I'd taught myself it was weak to cry and show any emotion which could leave me vulnerable, so I soon pulled myself together. I had also arranged for twelve red roses to be presented to Grace after the meal, so we ended up with twenty-four red roses! It was a wonderful day and evening full of joy and laughter, a very special time that would remain with us for ever.

CHAPTER TWO

Our relationship had developed quickly, and we experienced highs and lows in the following years. Our commitment in August 1994 and my birthday in February 1995 were both wonderful and will always be remembered as some of my favourite times. Although I knew initially Grace had been trying to help me, her attempt at counselling me and encouraging me to address my many issues from my past left me even more confused and had a detrimental effect on our relationship. Perhaps that is why Grace started to wonder and, in the end, started a relationship with a work colleague, who was also someone she already knew before we had met.

I turned a blind eye to this for some time, not wanting to accept what was happening and hoping it was just a fad that would pass. But as the weeks and months passed, I could see that Grace had no intention of finishing this affair and so I would have to deal with it in some way. I was still fighting with my emotions over my past, but I now had to deal with the betrayal by someone I had put my trust in so completely. I had allowed the brick wall built up over the years to be breached and it had left me exposed to all the hurt and betrayal I had felt as a child.

At the end of March 1997 I was questioning my ability to cope. The hurt and pain I felt at Grace's betrayal was all too real and genuine, what made it worse was the fact she made me feel guilty for my upset and confusion. Each day I tied to prevent my feelings from getting the better of me, but I was finding I could no longer hold back the tears in front of her.

Grace took the trust I had in her and abused it by having an affair. I know how much I frustrated her when I was not able to move on from my demons, despite her every effort to help me. I wonder now whether I would have been better never starting to reminisce and let the past stay in the past and concentrate on making a future with Grace. But it was not all my doing, Grace wanted me to delve into what had happened to me as a child and teenager, but it brought up so many bad memories, I wasn't able to process them in a meaningful manner. Trusting somebody and being trusted in return is the most important aspect of any relationship, without trust there can be no foundation to work from. I found as I began to trust Grace, the barriers began to break down. I was starting to have faith in how my life could transform, and how with trust I could have faith in a future which would be joyful and happy without the continual fear of being let down by those closest to me.

But Grace took away my trust in her, and any wrong I did to Grace I paid for by the deceit of her affair. Although she assured me the affair with Rachel had ended, she expected me to accept the fact that they worked together, and they would still be going for their Friday after work drinks. Her explanation was that she and Rachel had been friends for a long time, and the affair was just a fling, and it should not mean she should lose her friendship with Rachel. Grace told me I am not her keeper, and I can't control what she does or who she sees, so she will go for a works drink on a Friday, and it is my problem if I cannot accept her and Rachel having a social drink.

I was not trying to control Grace and I wouldn't stop her doing anything that she wanted to do, but her lack of compassion and appreciation of how this was making me feel did not allow me to start to regain my trust in her. I saw her anger directed towards me because of this lack of trust and the absence of any willingness to understand that she is being selfish in what she expected me to accept. She cannot see that there are far too many deep open wounds that need healing and while she insists on rubbing salt into the wounds, they are forever sore and weeping. She tells me that she loves me, but knowingly she continues to hurt me.

I don't know what I felt anymore, I was so confused, scared and there was an emptiness filling my soul which for once had been happy. For months I had trembled inside with my stomach being in a constant knot. Fridays were always the worst, feeling tense knowing that Grace and Rachel would be in the pub together, and wondering what they were talking about and whether they were still lying to me. Were they laughing at me and taking me for a fool? I felt the hurt and pain engulf me. Knowing that Grace was aware of how I felt and what she was doing to me just increased my anger.

On these Friday evenings, I would find myself getting hot, sweaty, crying, feeling sick and not able to keep still. I would pace the floor in the attempt rid myself of these feelings, but of course they just get worse. It became impossible to see things clearly or calmy or apply any reason to my thinking. I wondered why this friendship with Rachel meant so much to Grace that she wouldn't give it up to save my hurt. I questioned whether this friendship meant so much to her that she would take the risk of losing me? She wanted my trust and yet she couldn't see all the time she continued to hurt me she lost a bit more of me. Perhaps she was not bothered about our relationship and I had misread the situation, she seemed convinced I wanted to control her, but that was not true I just wanted a bit of understanding.

I had loved my mother once, but she broke my trust and continued to hurt me until I ended up hating her. Although I still loved Grace, the hurt was starting to take its toll and I was beginning to question what I was fighting for. I once loved Grace unconditionally, but I was beginning to find I loved and hated her in equal parts. There was nothing I could do to show Grace that I didn't want to control her, and Grace would not give up seeing Rachel socially to give our relationship the space to heal. I had decided I was not going to ask Grace to stop seeing Rachel, that would be unfair of me, but I would have hoped Grace would have seen for herself what she was doing, but I think she was blind to the effect of her actions, which worried me. Bit by bit my love was being destroyed by the pain and lack of trust I now felt for Grace. If anyone was going to put this right, it would have to be Grace.

I knew I would continue to hurt until my love for Grace ceased, at least then I wouldn't be tormented with self-doubt and haunted by the past. By her own actions, I don't believe Grace understands the meaning of love. I wouldn't dream of hurting her as she was hurting me. I knew in my heart I would not be able to cope for much longer. I told her so many times how I felt I was second best, and her friendship with Rachel was more important than our relationship, that I feared we would not last much longer if things did not change. I knew I should end it, but I was too weak and I kept hoping Grace would see how seriously this was affecting me. I am sure there are not many people who would accept their partner socialising with their x-lover, and yet this was exactly what Grace expected. I know if it had been the other way round, Grace wouldn't have allowed the situation to continue, so I question why she expected me to deal with it. She must have realised she was losing me, but it seemed her friendship with Rachel was apparently more important.

Logically I knew Grace and Rachel were no longer having an affair, although there was always that doubt in my mind that I was still being lied to. I had too much time on my hands which allowed me to continually think and analyse what was happening, and you blow things out of proportion. Perhaps I was overreacting but every Friday a little bit more of my faith was destroyed, by Wednesday I managed to control my emotions, but then would be building-up for Friday again. You learn to live with your emotions, but I knew come Friday my imagination would be running wild and I would simply want Grace to go away and never come back, and then maybe I would get some peace. I would never have hurt her but I hated her for how she made me feel. I had hoped these feelings of mistrust and lack of faith, which were so familiar to me in my youth, had gone for ever. But I found they were just below the surface and quickly resurfaced. How could she have expected me to feel the same towards her; how could she have expected me to say I love her and mean it with every ounce of body when I was hurting so much from the deceit, betrayal and continual confusion about her relationship with Rachel; how can you love someone when they are destroying your trust, your love and faith in human kindness? We had a chance to recover from Grace's affair, but she wouldn't take the opportunity because she accused me of trying to control her, when all I wanted was some consideration from her.

To rebuild a relationship after an affair is difficult and takes trust on both sides; while I desperately wanted to trust Grace, I felt there was nothing coming back and she could not see how unfair this was on me. Her refusal to change her friendship with Rachel was causing the death of our love. There was nothing I could do, it was down to her to deliver the remedy to save our relationship, but she categorically would not.

Grace had told me I could trust her one hundred per cent, but I can see I made a terrible mistake in believing her. Kelly had told me that her affair with Mandy was over and that they just wanted to be friends, but she lied to me as well and she ended up leaving and living with Mandy; how could I believe Grace was not doing the same? How could I believe what Grace says?

There were days when Grace did not want to go to work because she wanted to stay at home with me, and yet on a Friday she was always happy to go to work and then to the pub with Rachel. Her loyalties were confused. It also pains me to think that the two people who have wronged their respective partners have lost nothing, but in fact gained. Victoria (Rachel's partner) and me were the only two losers. Grace thought I was just feeling sorry for myself and wallowing in self-pity, but the hurt from again being lied to, cheated on and having my trust abused, was so great it ran through my entire body, made worse by the fact that I knew Victoria knew nothing of this affair, and she too was being deceived by the two of them.

Grace understood how much I loved my Dad, and how hurt I would have been if he had ever abused my trust in him, and because she knew I loved and trusted her, I don't understand why she could not comprehend how painful her deceit was. She also knew how much talking about my past had helped me deal with some of the suffering I have endured during my earlier years. I needed to talk about the current situation with someone, but as Grace was the sounding board for my recovery, it was impossible for her to be my mentor for this crisis as she was personally responsible for my suffering. But I knew I needed to talk and would so have liked to be able to sit down with Grace and have an honest discussion about the situation without it turning into a slanging match or hurling abuse at each other. I desperately needed my friend back, I felt so lost without her and missed how she used to be, caring and loving. She never judged me or called me stupid but always tried to understand me and help me if she could. Grace, of all people should have understood how I was feeling. She used to cry when I told her how something hurt me but now, she just calls me silly for having these feelings.

CHAPTER THREE

Eventually, Grace and I managed to talk, and I thought she understood and cared how I felt, but she didn't and in all honesty it made matters worse. She totally disregarded my feelings and I concluded that she didn't love me, maybe never did. She kept claiming her love for me, but no one can be so cruel if they love you.

In the early hours of the morning, I would find myself wide awake; my throat burning as I tried to hold back the tears. I would think about what the future holds for me, and it was not pleasant, as all I could see was loneliness and sadness ahead of me. Everything is so much worse at night, but all I could think of was how hard and uncaring Grace had become towards me, and how much attention she seemed to bestow on Rachel. I felt as though I wanted to die and get away from the suffering and pain, I had never felt so alone in all my life.

Looking back at those eighteen months my heart breaks knowing that Grace and I could have been happy, but unfortunately so many things had destroyed our loving, cherished, respectful and deep-seated relationship, there was no going back.

When you are feeling that low, you are tested daily in an act of self-survival to have the strength to carry on and not succumb to weakness which could take you down a very dangerous path. We argued daily, hurt and emotionally ripped each other apart. Although Grace's affair can directly be attributed to damaging our relationship, not all the blame can be placed at her door. It is never one sided and I must share some of the blame. I am under no illusion of my own faults and injustices that I have placed on Grace, but although they have substance, they don't compare to the severity of Grace's emotional cruelty towards me following her betrayal and ultimate affair with Rachel. Her abuse of the trust we had built up, had finally crippled me emotionally and that's when my strength was totally destroyed and I was left an emotional wreck, unable to function. This is when you are at your most vulnerable. You cannot see things for how they are and cannot look beyond the pain and hurt being inflicted on you.

Although I cannot wholly blame Grace, I believe she still doesn't comprehend the affect her actions have had on me. She thinks, she had an affair; it's over and we should forget it and move on with our relationship. But it isn't just the fact she had an affair, if it had just been that it would have been so much easier to have dealt with, it was the fact I lost my trust in people, my confidence in myself and something I had never had before, a true friendship.

There is suffering which is physical, which can be treated with medicine; there is suffering which leads to addictions or in identity crisis, both need treatment to help you to overcome your suffering and live a fulfilled life. But when you cannot get the help you need, it is difficult to recover and find your way out of your suffering which seems to smother you.

I was not feeling jealous, but had a feeling of complete isolation and loneliness, vulnerability and loss. I was emotionally more mixed up than I had ever been. I found my suffering so extreme, and I didn't know how to start to mend. I understand now how important it is to talk, and how it can help put things into perspective. By starting to understand yourself, you start to mend and find a peace of mind which allows you to find a path to recovery. But at the time I had no-one to talk to as my confident was the person causing me the pain.

For once in my life, I had thought I'd found someone I could trust totally. Grace had given me a friendship, and I was able to return it without hesitation. I had felt for the first time in my life a real sense of identity, that I was worthy of the love given by someone, and that I could love in return unconditionally. Such was my love for her, I thought she would never harm me.

Before, my safeguard would have overcome these feelings and I would have had my barrier to protect me, but I had let that barrier slip and now I have no strength left within me to fight. I felt I was a shadow of my former self which Grace had helped me to create, but had then destroyed.

I don't believe Grace understood the complexity of trust; from both a spiritual and personal perspective it gives the strength for change. Putting your trust in someone is the biggest compliment you can give; it allows barriers to breakdown and allows you to have new experiences. Taking that leap of faith can open a whole new world of opportunities. But when that trust is abused, the faith built up comes crashing down and the barriers go back up stronger and higher than ever.

Since the affair finished, Grace and Rachel saw each other as friends and started working together again.

Not an ideal situation for me to deal with emotionally, but Grace enjoyed working with someone she knew, which she said made it easier for her.

Grace told me not to worry, that she loves me not Rachel and her loyalty is to me. And yet some of our conversations, which I had asked Grace not to repeat had got back to Rachel. So, I question where Grace's loyalty lay. I saw their friendship growing more each day, making me trust her even less.

I started a conversation one night without any ulterior motive, I just wanted to talk, so I asked her who was the most sexually mature woman she had ever been with – perhaps we had both had a drink or two! Hesitating, she asked me what I meant. So, I said "the woman that knows what you want and is aware of your sensual feelings and needs." I suppose I expected her to answer either Rachel or me, but of course I hoped she would have say Shane. She asked if I really wanted to know, but proceeded to tell me that it was Rachel and continued to say "Well you didn't want me to lie did you?". Out of all the people she had had relationships with she chose Rachel with whom, if it was to be believed, she had only slept with on two occasions. I know I had asked for it, but her answer showed a lack of compassion for my feelings and a complete disregard for me. I felt I had been kicked in the teeth again, and I knew our conversation would be discussed with Rachel. Worst of all was the thought that I would be compared sexually to Rachel. Is it any wonder I felt so insecure and isolated, but I ask myself why on earth would I have asked such a question, surely, I was setting myself up for fall, especially as I knew Grace had no empathy for me and was not likely to show any compassion. But sometimes, when you feel that vulnerable it is almost like someone self-harming, you have the need to inflict pain on yourself and by asking such personal questions is bound to result in painful answers. When you are living in this nightmare, it seems impossible to see how you will ever get out of it. There was no one who could give me guidance or help me to understand the suffering I was experiencing and show me the path I needed to take to find spiritual peace.

I would wake each night in a hot sweaty panic which I couldn't stop. There was a sudden fear that overwhelmed me with every nerve of my body on edge. A lump in my throat becomes harder and bigger as I try to force back the tears engulfing my eyes. I try to stop the thoughts going around in my head, but I can't, all I see is Grace and Rachel as lovers and Grace telling me that Rachel is better than I am in bed. And yet part of me still wants to make love and for us to be close again.

One weekend, Grace told me she wanted to feel that closeness we had had, and could we try to start afresh, and although I constantly had Rachel on my mind, I agreed, hoping we could get our relationship back on track. The weekend should have been good as there were two days without any contact with Rachel, but I could not believe it when Rachel brazenly and unannounced turned up at the house for a coffee. Both of them acted as though it was the most natural thing and there had never been anything between them, and we were all just friends. My stomach flipped, with any hope of the healing time for Grace and myself gone, I reverted back to my withdrawn state, leaving them to their coffee, Grace making no move to dissuade Rachel from out staying her welcome.

I wished these feelings would go away and I could accept the situation, but it was like being constantly reminded of a dread of losing something which should be so special. I had loved Grace so very much and she was the only one who had listened to me and understand how I felt, but she became the catalyst for my current trauma.

CHAPTER FOUR

Monday 17th March 1997 I had got up feeling tired with the work I had done in the garden over the weekend, as well as feeding Ruth's ponies, but I sensed something had lifted from my mind and I had felt emotionally stronger.

Grace sat in the garden with me and for once listened to me. Whether she totally understood just how mixed up I really was I am not sure, but she said that she did. She listened and seemed genuinely concerned, and that in itself lifted my spirits. I now believe she did not think I was silly and appreciated how her affair affected me, undermining the trust I had placed in her. It is surprising how much closer I felt towards her by just having that recognition. Although I still hurt and knew it would take a considerable amount of time to recover, at least we were not arguing anymore and I had a part of my friend back who I had missed for so long. A re-building of our friendship could begin, I just hoped we didn't let each other down again.

April 1997

Rachel called at our house to say that her and Victoria had split up and she was looking for somewhere in Redditch to live. I think she was asking in a roundabout way if she could stay with us, but needless to say, that was not going to happen. It transpired later in that morning she managed to find a bedsit, so the next day Grace as the usual knight in shining armour, leant Rachel some bedding and helped her to move her things. She was back by twelve thirty, so we had lunch and Grace was about to go to work when she said she would be giving Rachel a lift to work as they both now lived in Redditch. My immediate thought was "here we go again", just as we were beginning to put our life back on track. Grace could sense my obvious concern, and told me that she loved me and stay cool and not to worry as it didn't mean anything. She could tell I was upset and assured me of her love and to have a beer ready for when she got home from work. When she got back from work, she tried her best to reassure me that nothing was going on between her and Rachel, but then told me she was going to take a beer round to Rachel's and have a drink with her for half an hour, as she felt sorry for her sitting in an empty room on her own. She didn't seem to think of me sitting in an empty house! and I was supposed to trust this woman. I was now so confused and I felt she was twisting my emotions again. I still loved this woman but she was destroying me bit by bit. Each day my trust was eroded, despite our attempt to get our relationship back on track, I found I had no respect for her, and the way she treated me showed she had no respect for me. I really felt our partnership had come to an end. I don't know any person who had been treated as I had, and now having to accept that your partner is seeing her ex-lover on a daily basis, and believing nothing was going on. Whose fool did they think I was?

And now that Rachel lived in Redditch my nightmares were about to become more intense. No doubt Rachel would knock at our door most days and Grace, doing her good Samaritan bit, would invite her in for meals and a coffee, arguing that I can't accept her going to Rachel's, so is it not better that she comes here. I was in a no-win situation before, but it was only going to be worse with Rachel living in Redditch. Grace could not, or would not see what this was doing to me and that my love was slowly turning to hatred. It was mental cruelty, and I was so tired, unhappy and depressed I could not believe I had been so foolish to allow myself to have trusted someone one hundred percent. I felt I would never be able to trust my judgement again, as I felt I had let myself down by allowing Grace to break down my defences.

Whether this was paranoia, but I was convinced that Grace was lying to me and so I travelled round every pub and park in the area because I was sure she hadn't gone to work and was with Rachel somewhere. I felt overwhelmed with emotion and so tired, I just wanted it to end and to have peace of mind, otherwise I was sure I was on the verge of a break down. I was worried and hurting so much, I feared I was being taken over by anger and hatred, and I did not want that to happen again. When you are in this situation, your mind becomes twisted, and you cannot see or think clearly. It eats away at you, occupying every minute of thought and turns love to hate, respect to contempt, trust to distrust and hope to despair, leaving you so confused it is impossible to know what is real. I asked myself how much longer I could endure this heartache? In this situation, you keep asking yourself this question, and although the answer is always the same, the solution is almost too painful to accept. And so, you keep torturing yourself, desperately wanting it to end but fearing the outcome. Although I didn't find them, it didn't ease the deep feelings of mistrust.

I worked myself up into such a frenzy one evening when Grace was going to Rachel's for a drink that she phoned me to ask me to go round. She told me although Rachel and Victoria had split, she loved me and didn't want the same to happen to our relationship, so to show there was nothing going on, would I please join them.

However, I was full of mistrust and suspicion, and although Grace told me she was trying, I could not trust her. I believed there was an ulterior motive to her actions, and even if she was being honest, too much had happened for me to trust her again, but still I was not brave enough to call time on the relationship even though there was no happiness in my life and I couldn't see it returning under the current circumstance, if ever.

Most days Grace would go to work and my stomach would be churning, which it had done for months. On your own, you almost lose track of time; each day seems to mirror the day before reflecting the pain you feel. I could not clear my mind to think logically as thoughts would conflict with each other leaving me in an even greater confused state. It began to affect my mental ability to function and carry out normal everyday tasks. I was in such a state I could no longer be bothered to do any housework; I didn't see the dust building up or the washing up that had not been done from the night before. This emotional imbalance affects your whole life, leaving you exhausted and dysfunctional

Grace told me from the start that she loved me and wanted our relationship to work. However, considering recent events, which include her staying the odd night with Rachel, I couldn't help but question every word she said. The whole situation was frustrating. I wanted to believe what Grace said was true, and part of me did, but at the same time I couldn't help but be suspicious. I would have loved more than anything for Grace and me to work, but I was unsure whether this was really what she wanted. I knew Grace was not a bad person, but the excitement of a new fling was just too much for her to resist. Perhaps that made her weak as there would be a repetition in future years of her failure to remain loyal to me and it would ultimately result in her leaving me for one of our friends. But at the time I wondered if I could risk giving our relationship a chance. I had to consider that Grace's affair was not the only problem, her drinking was increasingly becoming a problem which could not be ignored. She had drunk for such a long time, I was really concerned that if she didn't stop, she would do herself serious harm.

July 1997

Just a few months later I totally flipped, shouting, screaming, tearing things up, throwing things about, and even at one state, hitting my head. I can remember clenching my fists and hitting the wall several times.

When I sit calmly and reflect on my behaviour, I can see the past six months had emotionally tormented and destroyed me, resulting in one insane outburst. Months of talking, with repetitive promises and then lies from Grace and Rachel, were going nowhere and the situation remained the same.

The sheer frustration of my life had suddenly overcome my mental stability and physical awareness resulting in an outburst of both emotional and physical violence. I can remember the feeling of adrenaline rushing through my veins and although frightening, it felt like a drug rushing through my entire body. The more I lost my self-control, the stronger the adrenaline became. It acted like a drug and the more upset and angry I got, the greater the need for the adrenaline rush. It was a bit like an addiction; the adrenaline acting as a drug which fuels the ability to react to situations, and I found it made me more aggressive and violent. It wasn't a characteristic I liked, but it was as though my brain was in a fog and I couldn't stop the reactions although I knew they were wrong.

I recall one evening being at Rachel's flat with Grace, and there was a heated argument, at one stage Rachel held my wrists firmly as if to stop me from doing something stupid; I can't recall what was I threatening to do, but I can remember thinking, "If you don't let me go, I'll show you just how strong I am, and I don't want to do that, but at least you wouldn't be around anymore". I must have hit something because my hands hurt, my knuckles were swollen and bruised and yet the pain didn't correspond to the injury, in fact the physical pain was superficial to how I felt inside. I felt as though I had lost control of myself, and what frightened me was what I could have done because I had no control, no awareness of my actions and no comprehension of space.

Although physically I had the scars to show my violent outburst happened, it's a blur and like a half-forgotten dream. The following day, I could hardly believe I had acted like that. But it leaves you wondering what may have been, and I knew I needed to take control of myself.

Somehow the next few years passed, and although our relationship lurched from crisis to crisis, we stayed together with life taking on a routine; there were some good times, because despite everything, we had a lot in common. We both loved nature and enjoyed the garden, making changes so we could grow vegetables and have the pleasure of digging our own potatoes! Grace was still drinking, but sadly I didn't have the knowledge to help her kick the habit, and she would not accept that she had a problem.

Rachel and Victoria had repaired their relationship, and were together again, and we had during the years spent time with them; I felt it was better to form a friendship, which allowed Grace to socialise with Rachel, than to run the risk of them starting up the affair again, although I could not be sure it had truly ended.

January 1999

We were at a New Year Eves party and one hour into New Year's Day of 1999. Victoria, Grace & Sally one of our friends) had already gone to the car while I went in search of Rachel to say we were leaving. It did not take long to find her propping up the bar at the other end of the room. She had consumed quite a lot that evening, well we all had, but she more than the rest of us. As Victoria didn't drink, she usually offered to drive as she had that night.

Rachel's consumption of gin and tonics that night wasn't that different to her normal drinking pattern. She was well over the limit for driving, but thankfully this was one of the rare occasions she didn't intend to drink & drive.

In the five years that Victoria & Rachel had been together, I found it incredible that Victoria had no concept of the amount Rachel drank and that she often drove. Victoria could be very naive and gullible where Rachel was concerned. As for Rachel, she was very clever at hiding the truth regarding the amount she drank and many other issues which Victoria had no idea about.

I recall trying to tell Victoria about Rachel's drinking; I could have opened a can of worms with some the things I knew, but Victoria not surprisingly became defensive and protective about Rachel, so what was the point of stirring up a hornets nest and ultimately causing a rift in their relationship? Victoria's reaction was only natural, but it didn't stop me from feeling deeply saddened, especially when Victoria pointed out two bottles of drink that had hardly been touched, and had been there for several weeks, so how could Rachel have a problem with alcohol? Of course, she didn't know that Rachel kept a secret supply of drink upstairs which she knew nothing about. Rachel had been happy to brag about her deception to Grace, and how easy it was to deceive Victoria about her drinking and other things. I realised Victoria would never believe anything I said about Rachel, and Rachel was far too clever in covering her tracks for Victoria to be suspicious of her.

There was no point in telling Victoria that the deceit extended to Rachel chewing mints and gum to disguise the smell of alcohol after a night out, especially when she had driven. She told us she would sometimes act the fool when she got home to disguise she'd had too much to drink. It helped that Rachel was able to hold her liquor and so was able to convince the unsuspecting Victoria.

Rachel had lied to Victoria from the very beginning about her drinking and this meant that the pretence had to be kept up. Rachel couldn't admit to Victoria that I was telling the truth about her drinking, and that most of her nights out she drank around eight doubles and then drove home. If Rachel admitted about her drinking, she feared what other lies might come to light.

Unfortunately, Victoria saw Grace as the person with the drink problem, which of course was true, but Rachel also had a problem. I could understand Victoria's reaction because when Grace had too much to drink, she slurred her words and had verbal diarrhoea; Victoria believed that was how people were when they drank too much, but Rachel was not like that. Rachel would go quiet and withdrawn and act slightly agitated. Finally, she would become argumentative and could turn nasty. Through Rachel's deceit and Victoria's naivety, Victoria was not going to hear the truth let alone believe it.

It had been a good New Year's Eve party and although extremely merry, it was good to finish the evening conscious of my surroundings and with my senses still intact. Sadly, the evening didn't end in the happy New Year's tone we had hoped. I can't say I was surprised, but I was disappointed.

I got to the bar and Rachel and I stood face to face. She looked at me angrily and asked what I thought I was playing at. For a moment the question didn't make sense, but the more I thought back over the evening, I recalled I had received a few kisses from Sally, and I began to understand the meaning of her question. Her eyes smouldered which I could only assume was aimed at me. I also noticed a tearfulness, although within seconds that altered and her eyes became hard again. As if pulling a mask of deceit across her face she hid any emotion and without warning became cold, calm, and callous. I had seen this look before, and I had hoped I'd never to see it again, but unfortunately I was, and the alarm bells were ringing.

Rachel's recent behaviour had made me suspicious, but they were now heightened. She had admitted to Grace and me three years ago, that she had again become disillusioned with Victoria and by her own volition, she had not been happy since before their blessing. She confessed she only continued with the blessing because arrangements had already been made and she didn't want to hurt Victoria. Two other factors which had increased my suspicion were Rachel's obvious detachment from Grace, and her increased, and obsessive involvement with Sally. Although on a Friday evening we would all meet for a couple of drinks, Rachel would hint that her and Sally were going out later and in a subtle way it was always clear that we were not invited.

As we stood at the bar, still looking into each other's eyes, she said, "I am having an affair with Sally, but you already know that don't you?" I gave a silent nod of the head and she continued to tell me she knew there wasn't any future and it couldn't go anywhere. It was as if telling me made it more acceptable for her to continue with the affair, in some way justifying it.

And so, the evening ended with more deceit and lies to be carried forward into the New Year. I was in the unenviable position of knowing that Rachel was again cheating on Victoria, and not knowing how to deal with this knowledge. Should I tell Victoria or keep quiet and allow the deceit to continue unchecked.

For days after New Year I thought of nothing else. I was angry and disgusted with Rachel and concerned for Victoria who hadn't a clue what was going on. I had never wanted to find myself in a position of having to decide whether to tell Victoria about Rachel's deceit. This was a dilemma of trust, but I guessed in the end Victoria would not choose to believe me, she would side with Rachel who would no doubt refute any accusations.

It wasn't a question of where my loyalties lay, but whether Victoria would believe me, after all this accusation would have far more consequences on their relationship than saying about Rachel's drinking. As far as Victoria was concerned, Rachel could do no wrong and if by any chance Rachel had strayed, it wouldn't have been Rachel's fault but more the company that she had kept.

The position I found myself in, was to say the least, disturbing and the whole issue of my moral principles was being brought into question again. I had to find a satisfactory resolution to the predicament Rachel had again placed upon me. She knew my moral compass would make this very difficult for me, and I would be torn between telling Victoria or keeping quiet and being complicit in Rachel's secret. Perhaps she didn't care one way or the other, after all this wasn't the first time she had cheated, and I doubted it would be the last. Maybe perversely she wanted me to tell Victoria.

I was sensitive to the fact if I told Victoria, I had no choice other than to reveal the whole five-year saga, including Rachel's affair with Grace. I wondered if, when it came to it, I would have the courage to go through with it. I saw the consequences of the disclosure could have two serious repercussions. It could destroy Victoria's relationship with Rachel, and it could destroy our friendship which I would find upsetting as I had grown very fond of Victoria.

Victoria was very intelligent and I respected and looked up to her, but sadly she was in love with a women who had convinced her she told the truth. Rachel was the apple of Victoria's eye, and she could see no bad in her. But there was a bad apple lurking there.

I knew if I told Victoria, she'd want proof to collaborate my accusation; but where and how do you compile evidence about a liar and especially one who could easily make it appear I was simply taking revenge on her affair with Grace.

Victoria already thought I could be violent; an opinion she got from the many brutal arguments I had with Rachel at the time of her affair with Grace. As a rule, I am a placid person. I certainly don't look for trouble and it takes a lot to antagonise me, but when it does I can be aggressive and hot headed, striking first asking questions after.

This does not mean I condone violence, and there is very rarely a good reason to resort to physical harm. I am not trying to excuse my outbursts, but they were usually due to frustration when I found myself in a situation which I could not resolve, and I resorted to aggression. Some people are sufficiently articulate and can disarm a conflict with words; I could never do that as my vocabulary was never good enough to give me the armoury I needed, so ashamedly I depended on violence.

The question may well be asked as to how any sort of friendship developed between the four us on the back of Grace and Rachel's affair. The truth is Grace and Rachel had known each other for some time, and I had massive respect for Victoria, and a lot of the time we enjoyed each other's company. Once the affair had ended, it wasn't difficult for a friendship to grow. Whether this helped me or not I am not sure; at least when we were all together, I knew Grace was not with Rachel on her own, so maybe I got some comfort from that.

What shocked me was how quickly my mood could change; from enjoying a sociable evening, a wrong comment or look between Grace and Rachel and I would react, and inevitably it would lead to an argument which would end up with me throwing something or lashing out. I know Victoria was always shocked and surprised at my behaviour, and I felt I had let our friendship down, but still I pushed the boundaries to see how far I could go. I understand now this was all part of my lack of trust, and wanting to test any new friendship to see if it would break.

This was a chapter in my life I wouldn't wish to live through again and certainly I'm not proud of. By no means do I condone my actions but, in my defence, no one really understands their own capabilities until under duress, and I am sure that I didn't anticipate how I would react. I realise that the friendship between Victoria and myself could not be the same since my outbursts, which saddens me and made this whole situation much harder to deal with.

Lies, deceit, infidelity, I was fed up with the whole mess. I wondered why others couldn't be more like me, truthful and loyal to their partner. I realised my truthfulness could appear arrogant; I call a spade a spade, but at least people know where they stand with me.

I had, however, started to question my own standards. I started to question what truth meant and how it linked with trust. I knew I had a problem with trust, and that lack of trust had resulted in my barriers and finding myself isolated in a world I sometimes found difficult to understand. So, what comes first? Trust of Truth? If people do not tell the truth, how can you ever trust them? Had Mum been truthful and told me we had to move so often so she could work and support us, I would have understood even though I was a child. I would have trusted her, knowing she was acting in our best interest. But her lack of honesty led me to doubt her, and not understand why, yet again, I was being moved from my school where I had just started to make friends.

Can truth be clouded by personal interpretation? What one person may consider to be the truth may be challenged by someone else. While one person may say the weather is too hot, genuinely believing this to be true, another person may say the weather is too cool, also believing this to be true; so truth is subjective and can be interpreted by individual perceptions. So, when Mum decided not to tell me about the moves, did she do that truly believing it was better for me not to be told, whereas someone else may have truly felt it would be better to tell me – a subjective view. Unfortunately for me, Mum's decision was not the right one for me, but should I really blame her, perhaps it was done with the best intention. And now I must admit I have not always been truthful! I recall one incident when I was about twenty-three and in my first gay relationship. We were saving to go on holiday and had agreed to give up smoking to save enough money. Despicably I couldn't kick the habit having smoked since I was fourteen, and so I would go to our outside toilet and have a quick smoke, putting the butt on the top of the cistern! When my partner found out she was so disappointed with me, and my dishonesty. I learnt a valuable lesson from that, and it only went to enforce my belief in the importance of truth, even if you stray occasionally.

Sadly over the years the reliance on "your word is your bond" has diminished as it relies on truth, honesty and integrity, which seems to be lacking in today's world.

Truth can fill our lives with happiness, but conversely it can also cause pain and suffering. We are at times faced with the decision whether to tell the truth, or spare heartache and suffering by telling a lie. But to take the path of deceit leads to other suffering and torment, and so by staying with the truth no matter how hard it may be, must be the right choice. Whatever pain and suffering the truth may lead to, it can be faced, and in many cases can result in a positive outcome by recognising that suffering and dealing with it. Surely whatever the circumstances, and however hard it may be to hear the truth, it must be better to deal with the truth than live with a lie.

Lies can only come from self-betrayal and self-corruption, they are usually told because you want to impress or tell someone what you think they want to hear, or to avoid being honest with yourself. These lies have a way of haunting our minds and multiplying like a cancerous growth, they can overwhelm us with the need to survive and not lose face. A single lie is complicated and arduous to maintain, but it is of your own making so you bring suffering onto yourself; simply tell the truth.

Just after New Year, during one of our normal Sunday phone calls to Victoria and Rachel, that over the years had become a ritual, Grace asked Rachel, as she knew Victoria was in the garden, about the affair that she was having with Sally. Although I couldn't hear both sides of the conversation, it soon became obvious that Rachel was denying it. After the phone call ended Grace confirmed not only was Rachel denying the affair but was also denying even saying she was having an affair to me. Later that evening Rachel arrived at the house to continue with the discussion, wanting to make it clear that she was most certainly not having an affair. From her demeanour, what she was saying did not support her body language and I was convinced she was being deceitful.

There were too many things that didn't add up on New Year's Eve; on two separate occasions Rachel and Sally had disappeared for long period of time, far too long to be a visit to the Ladies, or order fresh drinks. I wasn't the only one that noticed their absence, both Victoria and Grace had commented. In addition, there had been marked flirtatious eye contact between the two of them, a look I recognised seeing during her affair with Grace. I knew I had not seen her looking at Victoria in that way for many years. This eye contact between Rachel and Sally wasn't something new, it had been going on for several weeks, but as the evening wore on and with alcohol dulling the senses, they didn't realise they were making it so noticeable. I had the last dance of the night with Sally, Grace wanting to sit it out as she was not feeling too good, and I was surprised when Sally turned to Rachel at the end of the dance and said, "I suppose you are going to give me a hard time now aren't you!" This remark obviously made me look at Rachel for some kind of conformation or denial; Rachel didn't say a word but the look of jealousy and anger said it all. If I were to now believe as Rachel wanted, that her and Sally was not having an affair and were simply just good friends, then the comment Sally made and the look from Rachel disputed this claim.

Within a matter of a few days, Rachel admitted to having an affair, and was now denying ever saying it. If Rachel was trying to convince me that nothing was going on, it certainly wasn't working. In her attempt to cover her lies, she had forgotten that lies only bring vulnerability and however hard she tried not to give the game away, sequence of events, cover ups, past history and her all too familiar cool attitude gave the game away.

I may seem revengeful when I say it angered me to think she was getting away with it, and Victoria was being cheated on again. Rachel could, until she had too much to drink, be good company, and be someone you could have a good time with. She could also be a thoughtful person, and I am sure one day will make a true commitment and I hope it is with Victoria. Unfortunately, until that time comes, if ever it does, she will remain a liar and sadly disloyal to friends and especially her partner.

My concern was for Victoria, I was not seeking revenge for her affair with Grace, after all it takes two and Grace and Rachel must share the blame for their

213

affair, but what she had done to Victoria and continues to do behind her back, not only angered me but proved Rachel's inability to be a genuine person. I have never felt a true connection between Rachel and myself; her attitude towards others and total disregard for their feelings stands in my way of ever forming a close friendship. In addition, knowing about Rachel's indiscretions and not telling Victoria, as well as my past violent outbursts towards Rachel, had also compromised any chance of a friendship.

Victoria had become the underdog and had been so for some years. She was an innocent, unsuspecting, good natured, generous person, but was in love with Rachel so was blind to Rachel's of infidelity and deceit. Although outwardly Victoria portrayed happiness, I had on many occasions a suspicion of an air of sorrow and disappointment and felt she portrayed an aura of abandonment which gave rise to my suspicions that she felt an overwhelming sense of isolation.

I am not on my own, finding myself in a position where I had to choose between being truthful about what I believe, or keeping quiet to keep the peace. I thought long and hard about what I should do, but decided I had to be truthful, even if it meant damaging our friendship. Telling Victoria my suspicions about Rachel, and her previous affair with Grace was hard and extremely emotional as it brough back the pain of Grace's deceit. I knew it was unlikely Victoria would believe me, and of course she didn't. As I suspected it put an end to our friendship, which was a high price to pay, but I had no choice. Years later, our friendship would be renewed, but at the time I felt I had lost a good friend in Victoria.

POST SCRIPT

Shane passed away before she could finish her book, and we decided it would not be right to take the liberty of attempting to finish it. This was Shane's story, and she told it from the heart. Other than Shanes' we have changed all of the names, as her writing is not intended to be an accurate description of anyone, but rather how various circumstances she found herself in affected her life and trust in people.

EPILOGUE

Grace and Shane did go their separate ways some years later. This was a double blow for Shane, and left her very bitter and absolutely devastated. Once again, she found herself in a difficult financial position, with the pressure of only one income to cover the bills. With some persuasion from friends, she registered with a dating forum for gay women, and subsequently met someone who she always said was the love of her life. They had a number of happy years together, enjoying their caravan down in the Forest of Dean, and making some good friends. They were able to extend the house, adding an extra bedroom and conservatory, and of course, Shane continued to grow vegetables and tend the garden. Steph was a worker and hated the fact Shane was burdened with debt, so she helped Shane to clear the outstanding loan and paid for the conservatory. Sadly, the relationship ended, resulting in Shane having to sell her family home and move to a new house, her trust once more damaged.

Shane was on her own for the last ten years of her life but had good friends who didn't let her down. She was always included in Christmas and New Year, Bank holidays, Birthdays and Special occasions. Most Saturday evenings were spent enjoying good food and drink with friends, playing cards which she usually won, or Monopoly when she showed her competitive nature! The biggest regret was that Shane did not meet someone to share her life with, who would have been there for her. Her daily phone calls with Sue helped to lessen the loneliness, but didn't replace the companionship of having someone special to share her life with.

Age mellowed Shane and she renewed close friendships with Grace, Victoria and Rachel, and she was very fond of them all and considered them to be good friends. Shane was our close friend and was always there for us, as were we for her. She often had a desperate phone call from us when one of the dogs disappeared in the park chasing rabbits, bringing coffees down as was waited for them to return!

Shane was always a deep thinker, in her later years she started to find some peace and to understand some of the reasons for her mothers' actions, and perhaps they were not intended to hurt her, but were just a product of the circumstances they found themselves in.

Covid was hard on her and like many people, it took its toll on both her physical and mental health. Although she kept safe during the covid years, she had repeated coughs, and was given numerous courses of anti-biotics. When she eventually had a face-to-face meeting with her doctor, she was sent straight down to A&E and admitted with serious breathing complications and was diagnosed with Pulmonary Fibrosis. Although she was discharged after a ten day stay in hospital, she had to have piped oxygen in the house, but passed away just two days after returning home.

This book is dedicated to Shane, she would be thrilled that it is in print. It is a simple recollection of her battle with trust, and how it affected her life. So many people let her down by abusing the trust she placed in them, perhaps that's why she didn't look for another relationship and was content with her own company.

www.ingramcontent.com/pod-product-compliance
Lightning Source LLC
LaVergne TN
LVHW011324080426
835513LV00006B/187